Concepting

Creating successful brands in a communication-oriented era

Jan Rijkenberg

www.warc.com

**World Advertising
Research Center**

First published 2001

World Advertising Research Center
Farm Road, Henley-on-Thames
Oxfordshire RG9 1EJ, United Kingdom
Telephone: +44 (0) 1491 411000
Facsimile: +44 (0) 1491 418600
E-mail: info@warc.com

Copyright © Jan Rijkenberg 2001
Translated by Andrew Buettner
Edited by Jim Adams and Wilbert Kragten

A CIP catalogue record for this book is
available from the British Library

ISBN 1 84116 090 3

Typeset in 10/13pt Sabon by Marie Doherty
Printed and bound in Great Britain
by Cromwell Press, Trowbridge

To my wife Mia, who enjoys my thought-juggling,
but always makes sure I keep my feet firmly on the ground.

In special memory of Janet Fontaine (1935–1993)

'Very inspiring. Not only to new start-ups but to established companies with established brands. We can all learn a lot from concepting's creative approach.'

René Hooft-Graafland
Director, Corporate Marketing, Heineken International

'A strong brand is not always a strong concept, but a strong concept is always a strong brand. This book explains how to develop concepts, something we at Diesel firmly believe in.'

Maurizio Marchiori
Director of Communications, Diesel

'Not often does one read a book when one comes across so much well-argued confirmation of what ones feels intuitively. This is one of those books.'

Frans Vogels
President, General Cigar International Ltd, USA

'If you want your brands to remain dynamic and survive...or if you want to find out how to develop new, successful ones, read this book: you'll learn a lot.'

Leo Witvliet
CEO, ETM Ernst & Young Netherlands

Contents

Chapter 1

Introducing Concepting

This book is based on the conviction that companies in many sectors are reaping the last benefits from traditional marketing and communication. Twenty or thirty years ago these techniques gave them an enormous competitive advantage. Today this is less and less so, since the vast majority of companies in any given line of business are using the very same marketing and research techniques and the very same communications means and tricks. The marketing competitive edge is disappearing.

Traditional marketing and communication techniques were, of course, very effective for many years. Indeed, companies that used them held pre-eminent positions in their markets, allowing them to fend off or elbow out weaker competitors. They were able to transform their products into strong 'brands' and acquire significant market share. As a result, many markets have become neatly crystallised: major brands are widely known and new brands surface rarely, while consumers are conveniently segmented into clearly defined target groups, each with its corresponding brand. However, the downside of this neat crystallisation is also clear: the markets have lost their dynamism – they have stagnated.

Now that most of the needs of the population of Western industrial societies have on the whole been more than satisfied – and indeed are practically stable – companies face the problem of maintaining sales and growth momentum. The main option, of course, is to grab market share from their close competitors – who, naturally, see things the same way. The result is a mutually destructive competitive spiral that has come increasingly to characterise the lives and survival strategies of companies. Marketing under these conditions becomes more and more an unimaginative, technical battle. In the process, companies lose sight of the actual needs of today's consumers, who are relegated to a secondary consideration in the battle for percentages.

When Kotler introduced the concept of marketing in 1956, his advice to companies was roughly the following: look at what is happening in a market, observe the needs, and then offer solutions to satisfy them.[1] Further differentiating oneself from the competition should be aimed at in a balanced 'marketing mix': a distinguishing product proposition, smart pricing, a choice of distribution channels and the formulation of the communication proposition. The four Ps – Product, Price, Place (distribution) and Promotion (communication) – were the simple ingredients for a successful approach to the market.

Significantly, the particular *sequence* of the Ps was not arbitrary; it indicated their relative importance: Product came first. This made eminent sense, since companies in the 1950s and 1960s were essentially production enterprises, offspring of industrialisation, concerned with providing the growing populations in Western industrial societies with a variety of new products and actually meeting real needs. There was obviously an enormous demand for all sorts of physical products to make life more comfortable. Any company putting a 'me-too' product on the market during this period of booming mass consumption could quite effortlessly profit from the strong demand for new products; this was the experience with innumerable products, such as vacuum cleaners, refrigerators and, more recently, fax machines.

Gradually many of these products reached the point where they could no longer be significantly improved upon. Today we have reached a situation in which investment in product innovation no longer strengthens consumers' preferences, because their basic expectations of a given product have already been met. Consumers are more than satisfied with the current offering and

---

1. P. Kotler (1956) *Marketing Management, Analysis, Planning, Implementation and Control.* First edition. Englewood Cliffs, New Jersey: Prentice Hall.

basically have no need for anything better. Some obvious examples of this phenomenon are products like detergents, tampons and nappies; but it is also increasingly occurring to more complex ones, such as automobiles and sound equipment. It is, in my view, very unlikely that a continued focus on product innovation by companies in such markets will produce satisfactory long-term returns. This, in a nut-shell, is because the approach demands greater and greater levels of investment in development and production, as well as in communication, the goal of which is to impose the renewed product on (already contented) consumers and getting them to purchase it.

This law of diminishing returns also applies, as we will see, in the case of brands that have sought to tempt consumers during the past couple of decades with 'added values', in a bid to gain a preferential position for their essentially generic products. Just as many products barely differ from each other intrinsically, so too have the 'promises' made in their communication become, with a few laudable exceptions, indistinguishable from each other. Just as companies continue to passionately 'innovate', so too does there appear to be a veritable obsession for ever-burgeoning communication budgets in a number of businesses that have reached their development limits. 'Outspend the competition!' seems to be their motto. However, is this entrepreneurship? Is this marketing? Or is it really an attempt to maintain a position of power at any cost; a case of wishful thinking for those who can (still) afford to wish?

Concepting offers companies a way out: a completely fresh and open approach. It steps away from the exhausting and claustrophobic battles fought by companies, armed with product propositions, for satiated, strictly delineated markets and target groups. Instead, as the name implies, it turns to the development of brands that embody *concepts* – a word I use in a broad and extensive sense. A concept goes beyond the product; indeed it is independent of the product. A concept is a rubric under which one could find visions, attitudes, convictions, philosophies, mentalities, motivations, 'wavelengths', areas of interest, world views and, indeed, whole 'worlds', which the brand elicits. However, even if concepts can be of different types and can be broader or narrower, what they all share is the fact that they actually *mean* something to the consumers; they evoke their sympathy and they even inspire them.

I felt I had to coin a new term because the existing terminology did not satisfactorily embrace the specifics of the phenomenon. 'Product development' itself is, of course, not appropriate because of its stress on product. 'Brand development' is also inadequate, because it is commonly used to refer to the process of developing names for new products for companies emerging from traditional processes, e.g. after mergers, that is, in situations where there is an existing product or service, for which a brand name or added value has to be developed. 'Concept development' could not be used because, in the world of communication, it is too often employed to refer to the development of an advertising or communication concept. The term concepting *seemed the most appropriate to describe the continuous process – not a one-shot, brand-invention exercise – which, as we will see, encompasses a concept's birth, development and ongoing nurturing, or management.*

The goal of concepting is therefore the creation and management of what I call concepts and the related *concept brands*. Nike is an outstanding example of such a brand. For the consumer, Nike is not simply a training shoe. It is a lot more: it represents an entire mentality – a 'world' of persistence, self-confidence, aspiration and performance.

From a concepting perspective, a target group is no longer strictly defined in terms of buying habits or sociodemographic factors. A new concept brand elicits a *new* type of buying behaviour. It creates what I call a *following*, since its 'supporters' identify with the brand intensely.

In light of the powerful personal identification they elicit from their following, concept brands take on many of the characteristics of a quasi-religious movement. Think back to the magnetism of Apple in the early 1980s (today undergoing a revival). Or think of Benetton, BSO (before becoming BSO/Origin), Nike, Virgin, The Body Shop, Smart, Caterpillar, Calvin Klein, Hugo Boss, Greenpeace, the Discovery Channel, Ben & Jerry's, Diesel and Swatch. Not only relatively recent brands come to mind: think of classic concept brands, such as Marlboro, Peter Stuyvesant, Club Med, Disney and Davidoff. In all these cases, buyers and brands reinforce and affirm each other, creating a strong underlying sense of mutual solidarity between brand and following.

Concepting thus differs greatly from 'positioning' or 'repositioning',[2] as we will see in Chapter 5. These approaches tend to apply to brands that have been around for decades and are owned by companies that began as production enterprises and then became (or added) sales organisations. Such companies have used *marketing-oriented* techniques for the last 30-odd years to boost production and sales figures. In this type of battle there is hardly any room left for profiting from product improvement. Since prices are market determined and demand is saturated, companies use the (frequently overrated) tool of communication as the only remaining lever: as a last resort.

Concepting, in contrast, entails a profound belief in communication as *the* means of sustaining the brand: as a first resort. Right from the very beginning, stress is placed on communicating the brand's concept. In fact, the concept is implicitly 'positioned' at the brand's very conception! No need to dream up added 'values' for positioning later on – not to speak of *new* ones, as in the case of repositioning. Instead, new *products* can actually be added under the concept brand, within its *concept field*. Boss has, for example, since its conception, incorporated a number of products, such as ties, shoes, aftershave and underwear. Soon, we will probably see Boss briefcases, wallets and jewelry.

Businesses that are guided by their concepts I refer to as *concepting companies*. Their management philosophy gives concepts a paramount position, as discussed in detail in Chapter 10.

---

2. First introduced by A. Ries and J. Trout (1981) *Positioning: The Battle for Your Mind*. New York: McGraw-Hill Inc.

All else is subordinate to them, be it production (often out-sourced), pricing (seldom low-end), sales or distribution. These companies never hesitate to adjust these variables if the development of a concept so requires.

In the terminology of the four Ps framework, one could view concepting as marketing 'in reverse'. The process does not begin with the Product, followed by the other Ps, which gain increasingly in importance (or become more necessary) over time. It actually begins with Promotion – that is, communication. After all, visions, attitudes, convictions, motivations, mentality fields and other concepts can only thrive by means of communication, which is how the world of the brand manifests itself in society. The remaining Ps, depending on the priorities set by the concept, are employed as tactical tools in a particular sequence. The manner in which this occurs reveals something about the concept's nature.

Although concepting companies are communication-oriented, this does not necessarily imply that they communicate *intensively*. As we will see later on in Chapter 8, it is more a matter of communicating appropriately and consistently, which actually often means *less* communication in the classical sense of the term

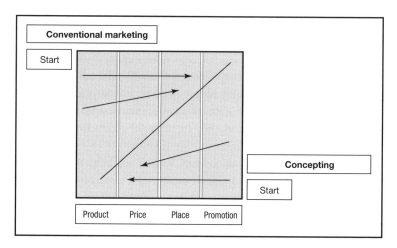

Figure 1.1 Concepting reverses the four Ps framework. For the sake of simplicity, we use the (outdated) terms 'Place' and 'Promotion', though they are equivalent to 'Retail' and 'Communication', respectively.

(i.e. media campaigns). Also, not only what the brand does and says in order to get its concept into the limelight is important, but also what it does *not* do and say. Ultimately, whether the brand communication – in *all* the brand's behaviour – is consistent with its concept will determine whether or not the concept 'clicks' with the consumer.

Concepting companies are organised and managed differently from conventional companies. They tend to be quite small, since the production of the physical product is often outsourced. They are made up of a compact, clearly defined *concepting team* which is dedicated, heart and soul, to the concept. All those involved are very well attuned to what people want. As individuals, they are also communication-oriented – that is, they are excellent communicators, which of course has little to do with having studied communication. Typically they are also highly entrepreneurial generalists, boasting capabilities in a number of fields.

Concept brands therefore tend to flourish less in traditional companies, in which the focus is on the production process. This is because such brands can only develop if a concepting team is completely free to create and develop its own vision unhampered by historical, production mind-sets and cultures. Often the only option for a traditional company is to set up a separate concepting company to develop these brands. Indeed, concept brands frequently flourish only because their creators succeed in wrestling free from the rules and rigidities of a company, and take responsibility for the realisation of their own concepts – Apple's Steve Jobs and Diesel's Renzo Rosso are good examples here.

In this context, companies that annually spend small fortunes simply trying to maintain the position of their conventional brands, and, in the process, bang up against the law of diminishing returns, might seriously consider establishing a concepting budget. They could begin by allocating 5% of their current marketing resources to a concepting team to develop ideas. Such funding would likely be minimal compared to the millions swallowed up by product innovation efforts. (Detailed ten steps to setting up concepting teams are discussed in Chapter 6.)

It is my belief that most consumer product and service companies will, in any event, increasingly be persuaded by the need, or obliged, to make a transition to concepting in the years to come. In fact, as we will see throughout this book, there is much evidence that this is already happening, as they realise that new concept brands are increasingly capturing the imagination and the loyalty of consumers, having sidestepped the classically defined markets.

The experience of many brands with deep historical roots is reminiscent of that of ancient oak trees. Both have owners who go to unimaginable extremes to try to keep them alive as long as possible. The oaks are sawed, pruned, trimmed, grafted and even given injections in an attempt to rescue them. In the process, the rescuers step on and crush young saplings and other types of trees that could have sprouted and grown up in the old oak's shade or in its immediate vicinity. These efforts succeed only in producing an arid circle of ground around the old oak, which finds itself increasingly isolated. Meanwhile, the rescuers stand around in a circle, backs facing the outside world, nervously fixated on their tree, anxious to see whether their efforts prove effective. From the corners of their eyes they give each other encouraging glances. 'He's going to pull through, don't you think?' Their companions nod in agreement. 'This time it's really helping.' No one dares to cry out: 'Who cares if the oak drops dead?!'

Chapter 2
Why Concepting is Necessary

The reason why concepting is necessary in many sectors is simply because the current systems are exhausted: they no longer provide companies with the growth they want nor do they provide consumers with the products and services they want. The signs of this exhaustion are not hard to find.

2.1 Existing markets are saturated

During the post-war period, when companies were predominantly production or sales oriented, they slowly came to the realisation that markets could actually become saturated. However, given their orientation, they simply (and often successfully) responded by seeking out other geographical markets. Many of today's multinationals, such as Unilever, Philip Morris, IBM and Philips, expanded internationally when confronted with the saturation of their home markets. They established sales, distribution and sometimes production structures in the new markets, where their sales-oriented approach was more than enough to guarantee success, particularly if they were the first on the scene. Products that met clear needs quickly found their way to the consumer.

Nowadays, however, most Western industrial markets have been penetrated and are increasingly becoming saturated. The very high growth rates attained through good salesmanship suddenly can no longer be taken for granted. This time, the companies in a number of sectors have responded by embarking on mergers and acquisitions, in an attempt to maintain or acquire market dominance.

Mergers and acquisitions are carried out within and without national and sector borders. Most of the time, however, they occur within a single line of business, such as the Martini/Bacardi and Compaq/Digital examples. Years ago, in the Netherlands, Heineken bought its competitor, Amstel, and recently, after having earlier missed the boat in the race for 'speciality' beers, succeeded in purchasing smaller breweries such as Brand and de Ridder. In the world of finance, the takeover spree has taken a bit longer to gain momentum, but is now fully under way. Stories of banking and insurance company mergers are headlined almost weekly in the media. The result: mega-companies.

However, is the creation of such mega-companies at all motivated by consumer needs? Are they offered better goods and services as a result? Are they offered new and better products or services, or do they still face the same limited choices character-ised by mass appeal and standardisation? I suspect the answer is, unfortunately, no. Indeed, the driving motivation behind the merger strategies seems to be cost reduction and the attainment of the power and size needed to be a 'significant global player'.

Sympathetic voices often portray the takeovers as a huge step forward for these companies. I feel that, from the perspective of the consumers in any case, and in light of the need for more sensitive, dynamic, imaginative marketing to meet their needs, it represents, at best, a huge step sideways. Naturally, it creates larger companies, but size does not necessarily transform these companies into the marketing organisations they need to be to ensure their ultimate success.

True, many companies have set up marketing departments in their head office and operating companies, but they are usually simple extensions of the production and sales departments. Further, innovations and sales targets are largely centrally determined. The same is the case with communication, from overall strategy to detailed execution.

Apart from the quest for size, many mega-companies have been mesmerised by another sacred cow: profitability through cost cutting. Instead of pursuing profit by creating services and products resulting in greater consumer benefits, they do so by taking the scalpel to the organisation. Further, they busy themselves dividing companies into 'profit centres' – even the mail-room is expected to turn a profit. The kudos goes to those who come up with ways of cutting costs. Furthermore, what happens to those who call for substantial investments in new product concepts to generate future profits? They are lucky if they're given any hearing whatsoever, let alone the funding and a chance to actually seriously develop their ideas.

As a result of these initiatives, many companies have indeed enjoyed high profitability and their stocks have performed accordingly. Closer analysis, however, shows that in many cases these results are not based on producing more value for the consumer, but on:

- Growth in new geographic markets
- Cost-cutting measures
- Lay-offs
- Acquisitions
- Book-keeping profits from real-estate sales

The concern with the bottom line has therefore had a positive impact, in the short term. However, though profits and share prices have soared, is this cause for celebration when sensitivity to the customer has not been improved? Take Philips, for example. Have all the years of downsizing and reorganisation led to more effective marketing operations? Have they improved the company's market positions in the various countries where it is active? Has Philips come up with new, successful product concepts for future growth and profits? Such questions attract few straightforward answers at the company's press conferences.

The authors of *Competing for the Future*, Hamel and Prahalad, have, with good reason, seriously questioned the trend towards one-sided downsizing and rationalisation.[1] They sketch an eerie

---

1. G. Hamel and C.K. Prahalad (1994) *Competing for the Future*. Boston: Harvard Business School.

scenario of companies that have been cut back to the bone. The minimal staff left are so demotivated and exhausted by all the reorganisations, that they can no longer muster the energy to work for their company's future. In the authors' words, the company begins to suffer from 'corporate anorexia'.

2.2 Market shares are saturated

It is quite striking how corporations tend to maintain their concentration on their existing product groups. Striking and puzzling, because these cash-cows are being milked dry, while new cows are seldom being bred – new star products are rare. This, I feel, is very revealing of the nature of much management philosophy today, with its obsession with organising, reorganising and merging. In addition, there is a frenetic competitive urge to be the market leader, or, at the very least, to maintain market position. Something of a herd-thinking prevails: everybody wants to be number one.

The desire to establish a position is of course understandable, but when it becomes an obsession – a goal unto itself – maybe it has gone too far? Companies have to take a step back and ask themselves some questions. For example: How much sense does it make to continue thinking only in terms of growing market share, when it is obvious that the competition is doing the same? Why engage in a bloody struggle for the last few bits of market share when they are far from the most profitable? Who really benefits when, for example, Unilever, Henkel and Procter & Gamble battle over market share? Does the traditional perception of the market really still provide the right approach?

More specifically: Why not be satisfied with the current market position and in the meantime – not later, which might be too late – develop new concepts? These could be in other markets, or even in newly created markets. Companies too often have their priorities reversed: instead of fighting over market share, they should focus on developing concept niches which will, as discussed later, determine the market share they ultimately acquire.

2.3 Consumers want new experiences

The behaviour and expectations of today's Western consumers can no longer be encompassed by market-share thinking. In this communication-oriented age, consumers are very savvy; they are nobody's fools and they demand respect. They are also becoming increasingly individualistic and want brands and products that enhance their personal identities. By definition, products that everybody owns become uninteresting. Consumers are also less and less willing to accept decreed lifestyles – they want to create their own worlds ('this is me') by selecting and combining all sorts of styles. The premis of mass consumption is shifting from 'each with the same product' to 'each with a self-selected array of concepts'. Quality and meaning are becoming much more significant than quantity or even price, which has long lost its differentiating competitive power.

Let us take an example of a company that failed to grasp this reality. In the early 1980s, Sara Lee/DE launched tea line extensions under the Pickwick brand in an effort to increase consumption and its market share. Complementing the already longstanding Pickwick 'English blend', it introduced an enormous variety of teas, particularly fruit-flavoured ones. The strategy met with initial success but is now reaching its limits. As the company racks its brains inventing new flavours and thereby promotes the further fragmentation of the market, it increasingly has to struggle with questions like: Who is the target group for the new apple–apricot flavour? How do we reach this target group through the media? Which flavour should we drop if supermarkets have no extra shelf space for a new variety? What does apple–apricot contribute to profits? More ominously, what should we do if (or when) retailers decide to copy these simple products and sell them for a few pennies less, using their own brands and the best shelf space?

The problem with such a strategy, despite its initial success, is that it is inward looking, amounting to little more than introducing 'cosmetic' product innovations under a single brand name. Also, as paradoxical as it might seem, all these tea varieties, ostensibly designed to give everyone a 'moment of personal tea enjoyment', under one brand name and with a clearly defined packaging concept, are actually counterproductive. They in fact undermine any real individuality, since the power of the ensemble, the package, overwhelms the individuality of the flavour.

An alternative, outward-oriented, concepting approach to tea marketing is increasingly being taken by some tea and coffee specialist stores, where one can choose from dozens of different teas and coffees (and have the latter blended to taste). In a setting of large sacks of coffee and tea tins and boxes with an old-fashioned copper scale on the counter, tea is sold in its most authentic form. Besides the *no-brand* teas, the stores also offer superb teabags from chic British tea companies and exotic Indian suppliers, and a wide and colourful selection of tea paraphernalia, from pots and strainers, to cups, saucers, cosies and warmers.

What these stores sell is the concept of individuality and mystique. The sort of 'tea experience' that captures the imagination of, and appeals to, the consumer who already has everything. With one's box of tea, one takes home the atmosphere of foreign and exotic cultures. In so doing, one makes a statement – both to oneself, comfortably on the sofa, cat-in-lap, and to others, with whom one wants to share this newly discovered experience.

What a contrast with Pickwick's apple–apricot approach! In response to these successful tea experiences, Sara Lee/DE will have to develop its own new, *meaningful* concepts to ensure future growth. These should not carry the Pickwick name – the brand is already typecast – and might even require completely different distribution channels than those classically used for tea.

That Sara Lee/DE is up to this task has been demonstrated in its successful creation of a completely new market on the basis of its ice-tea concept. This is an entirely new concept in which tea is (merely) a raw-material component: what really mattered was the experience it elicited. Initially, the introduction fell short of expectations because the communication was too closely related to the traditional context of tea drinking, and the consumer perceived the new product simply as 'tea gone cold'. However, by changing its tack, and communicating the *meaning* of ice-tea as a sporty, non-alcoholic, non-traditional soft-drink for adults, the company succeeded in appealing to a group of people for whom, for example, the (alternative) isotonic sport drink at the tennis club was a little too much.

Perhaps it was actually not such a bad thing that Sara Lee/DE's ice-tea success had such a bumpy start. The learning process will probably strengthen the company's realisation that it is indeed possible to come up with new concepts, regardless of what raw materials are involved.

2.4 Old brands have had their day

The life cycle of products is frequently discussed in marketing literature. In essence, the cycle here refers to the evolution of a product's consumer groups: at first, a small group of 'innovators' try the new product (usually relatively high priced), then the 'early adapters' acquire it, followed by the 'early majority', the 'late majority' and, lastly, the reluctant 'laggards'.

Although the entire life cycle is dealt with comprehensively in the literature, it seems that many organisations are determined to ignore the reality of the last, laggard phase. This is perhaps understandable. When companies, having gone through the early painful phase in which costs far exceed benefits, finally start enjoying high returns, selling the product to the early and late majorities (and the share of marketing costs of total costs is at its lowest), they are naturally reluctant to face the implications of the impending reality of the last phase. In other words, it is difficult to accept that the product has had its day and it is time to move on to new ones.

When the company, as seen earlier, starts investing increasing amounts in order to maintain minimal sales and market positions, the situation becomes dangerous. At this point it often attempts repositioning, fiddling with package designs, aggressively promoting the product on shop floors, and even producing it under 'private labels' for other companies. At most, such moves keep shareholders happy, for a while. In reality, however, they amount to little more than a stay of execution.

This reluctance to accept reality is bolstered by the fact that the tactical details of a company's marketing activities tend, in this phase, to be delegated down to the organisation level where the 'new kids on the block' are busily trying to make a splash to promote their careers. Every keen newcomer seems to come up with completely fresh and new repositioning proposals and sales-driven marketing plans. At the same time, the company might also bring in newly contracted advertising and sales-promotion agencies (or new teams within the existing agency), who quite cheerfully play along in this expensive wishful thinking. 'The previous campaign', they tell the client, 'had room for improvement: we can do a lot better!' Instead of recognising that the ship is doomed, company's spend energy and resources in a process equivalent to rearranging the deck chairs on the *Titanic*.

I must confess that I too have been guilty of this. I was swept along in this repositioning maelstrom for a number of years. Is there anyone with a few years of marketing experience who hasn't been? I have helped reposition brands up to three times over a period of a couple of years. As if personalities can be altered just like that! As if consumers will automatically understand and swallow it all!

I now believe that if repositioning for a particular brand is to work at all, it can only work every 10 years or so; this, providing all available resources are fully concentrated on the effort, as, for example, was done in the case of Bacardi. In the 1980s and early 1990s, Bacardi was the fun-on-the-island drink. Its communications showed only beautiful young people enjoying themselves, drinking the rum on a sunny island: a world most only dreamed of. It worked apparently. However, in the mid-1990s the attitudes of consumers changed. Instead of focusing on lifestyles, people became more individual, more inwardly driven, and thus demanded new attitudes from their brands. Bacardi sensed the change. It repositioned its Bacardi brand completely, from the fun-on-the-island to the island of its origin: Cuba. The company concentrated all resources on Cuba as the Bacardi bat logo proliferated. In doing so, Bacardi provided a good example of how brand repositioning can work.

However, the process can be overdone. There are innumerable examples of companies going against their better judgement and trying to stretch the life cycle of a product. How many times have we not read about the repositioning of 7-Up? New, clear and refreshing! Or take Levi's...

One doubts whether those in charge had done an adequate job of really studying the behaviour of this younger target group. Younger people simply are not interested in a drink that their parents like. Each generation creates its own culture with its requisite subcultures. Once something has become 'out', it is almost impossible to restore it to its previous 'in' status.

Several years earlier a similar scenario had taken place involving sherry. Corporate campaigns, no matter how attractive and contemporary they might have been, were unable to turn the tide in this case either. Realism is in order. Companies need to realise that an irreversible end to a given product's, product category's or a brand's popularity is quite possible. The fact that the company has built up all the facilities to produce and distribute it should not blind it. There are hundreds of new options available, but first the new concepts need to be developed.

Chapter 3

From Product Development, via Brand Development, to Concepting

Concepting is premised on the idea that brands are introduced to the market on the basis of particular concepts. In the evolution of business, concepting represents the latest phase, following the material-based, product-development phases, which still characterise most businesses at the end of this millennium. In short, businesses increasingly offer their customers intangible values.

There are in my view three successive product-development phases, each of which has a corresponding type of business organisation:

(1) Genuine product development (production-oriented organisation)
(2) Genuine product innovation (sales-oriented organisation)
(3) Cosmetic product innovation (marketing-oriented organisation).[1]

---

1. See Evolution of Entrepreneurship table on page 115.

3.1   Genuine product development

The archetypal product-development scenario that springs to mind is of a garden shed where the mad genius invents something as other-worldly as a light-bulb or telephone. Adapted to another setting, the image is not so romantic or inaccurate, because for years – certainly since the advent of the industrial revolution – product development based on human inspiration, raw materials and technology has led the way in the Western world.

Indeed, in a number of new lines of business, such as telecommunications and computers, this is still the case. Product development in such industries is a result of constantly advancing technological inroads and possibilities, which effectively lead to the invention of new products. The CD, CDI and CD ROM – all invented in Philips' Natlab – and products like vacuum-packed, pre-baked bread, electric toothbrushes, microwave ovens, colour printers, internet starter packages or migraine medicines are other examples. Such products still offer consumers something genuinely new, as did the first vacuum cleaners and refrigerators in the past. They are functional, tangible, 'from-the-factory' products. If they are affordable in relation to the new convenience or pleasure they offer, they quickly find their way to the consumer without the help of costly communication.

Such product development results in products that are firstcomers on the market: nothing comparable existed before; they are not variations on a theme. This is the category of products that have a genuinely distinctive 'Unique Selling Point' until, of course, the competition succeeds in copying them – nowadays, this can be a matter of a few months.

In the technologically intensive industries, new product development is usually led by the company's R&D labs. The disadvantage of this is that the developers get carried away; they get ahead of themselves and develop products that consumers are not, and may never be, ready for. Consumers sometimes find the utility of the products questionable – e.g. electric bread knives, high-definition TVs, remote controllers with 56 option buttons (and indecipherable and overly complex user handbooks) or automobiles capable of doing 280 km/h, even though the driver usually never gets out of second gear.

Such technical overkill is usually characteristic of companies run by management that has (too) much affection for the R&D lab and has lost touch with the outside world. This can produce disastrous results. It can happen that tens of millions of pounds are invested in new product lines, after which the new product, following a fitful introduction on the market, winds up in the company's flop collection.

Despite this threat, product development and organisations of this type are clearly required in sectors where the development of genuinely new products is called for. There will naturally always be companies dedicated to this task.

The distinguished feature of genuine product innovation is that the products are original and unique: nothing like them existed on the market before.

3.2   Genuine product innovation

After the first-generation products have established their position in the market, products containing genuine innovations start to appear. The business organisations producing these are similar to the original product developers. The innovations improve on the existing products or involve variations on them, and consumers find them very enticing when they need to replace their first-generation products. Examples of such innovations are, of course, multiple and can be found in every sector: lightweight vacuum cleaners with extra attachments; CFC-free refrigerators; steam irons; colour televisions; mobile phones; mercury-free thermometers; deep-freeze vegetables; sugarless gum; creams for dry skin; oily skin and everyday use; sun-screens with wide-ranging protection factors; and so on.

The ideas for the innovations in this phase no longer originate primarily in the R&D labs, but in the sales-force. The men and women who have direct contact with the consumer become the focal point for customer-sensitive innovation. Information from the sales front is then passed back to the lab. The process is, of course, not always smooth, since product engineers might baulk at some of the suggestions. Engineers who are particularly fond of steel, for example, might find the notion that a lightweight vacuum cleaner be developed using synthetic materials laughable, if not insulting.

Consumers are likely to take to these improved products quickly. Because the innovations meet manifest (rather than latent) needs, the consumer will, assuming the price is right, readily embrace the improvements for their convenience and the product's improved performance. The process is, of course, greatly facilitated by the fact that the producer usually discontinues production of the old product versions.

In many of today's markets, however, it is doubtful whether a business can gain or maintain a solid foothold with a strategy based on genuine product innovation. Competitors' copying capabilities are faster than ever, quickly rendering the 'new and improved' label meaningless. It is even doubtful whether spending small fortunes on communicating these 'Unique Selling Points' makes economic sense. No sooner has the innovation caught on with the consumer than the direct competition has already come out with its own version – e.g. the 'steam-burst' feature in irons, or the clever, under-the-cover stowing of vacuum cleaner attachments. Innovations of this sort are easy to copy. Extensive and expensive communication campaigns do just as much good for the imitators' products as they do for the innovator's.

The distinguishing feature of genuine product innovations is that they are also experienced and appreciated as such by the consumer: they are the reason the product is bought when the time comes for a replacement purchase.

3.3 Cosmetic product innovation

The strong attachment to the certainties of the past lie behind the phase I call *cosmetic* product innovation. Technically speaking, this is when the product's life cycle is coming to an end and management, driven by a product-oriented culture, continues to view 'innovation' as the only way to hold on to market share.

Since, over the past 10 to 15 years, consumers in a growing number of product categories are more than satisfied with the array of selections on offer, cosmetic innovations have become increasingly apparent. Companies spin these off at amazing rates: every successive 'relaunch' is backed by insistent, big-budget advertising campaigns. Winged sanitary towels are a good recent example of this: 65% of women consider the feature ludicrous! Other examples are hospitalisation insurance with a £1000 deductible clause, or, in the mid-1980s, 'his' and 'her' nappies followed, several years later, by the launch of the revolutionary invention: 'unisex' nappies! The memorandum on the following page typifies this mindset.

Like peddlers, brand-name producers hawk their cosmetically changed products, as if they actually believed their own 'improved', 'renewed', 'even more delicious' and 'improved performance' claims – not to speak of the incomprehensible chemical terms for ingredients to keep up innovation (and technical progress) appearances: 'now with "zeobisilene" for even *whiter* teeth'.

Often the cosmetic innovation consists simply of a different kind of packaging, which provides the distinctive-feature ammunition for a massive consumer offensive. 'Now with resealable cap'; 'Now with a pump trigger'; 'Now in liquid form'; 'Now in *non*-liquid form'; 'Now in 50-ml size'; and so on. In the case of food products, cosmetic innovation manifests itself in a variety of ways, including a cornucopia of fragrances and flavours, churned out at a dizzying pace. We have already referred to the Sara Lee/DE approach to teas, but such examples can be found in every sector – two of my favourites are peppermint-flavoured coffee and mixed peanut butter–chocolate spread.

The division of products into 'light', 'medium' and 'heavy', according to calories or alcohol content, or, on the basis of 'moment marketing', into 'morning', 'evening' and an endless variety of 'atmosphere moments', has attracted the attention of brand-name producers intent on securing an extra 'facing' on the retail shelves. However, the truth is that these divisions and moments are all too often very transitory. Indeed, the great open secret in marketing-land is that the vast majority of these

Memorandum

To: *Management Board Members*
From: *Director of Marketing*

Re: *Upgrading Yoghurt Line*

Over the past few weeks, indicative market research suggests that there are promising prospects for our new 'Midnight Yoghurt'. Seventy-two per cent of housewives say they will certainly try the product as soon as they see it on the shelves (market researchers hardly ever come across a score this high in this product category). Consumer preference tends more towards the 500-ml than the 1-litre package, since the product would seldom be consumed by more than two people at a time. In terms of price perception, consumers indicate that they would find a unit price of $1.89 for the 500-ml package reasonable.

Buyers for two leading retail chains have responded very positively to Midnight Yoghurt: they have promised a 6-week trial run in 40% of their stores, on the condition that we place half-page advertisements in their consumer magazines.

Assuming a 20% penetration of the target group (see preceding note) after six months, a repeat behaviour comparable to results achieved with 'Bulgarian Raison' and a weighted distribution of 45%, we estimate a 20% growth in volume of our yoghurt line as a result of the new introduction. This amounts to a 22.7% market share in Nielsen Jan/Feb in the 'speciality yoghurt' segment, giving us market leadership.

Now that the introduction date has been set, we will brief our advertising agency so that they can start with campaign development, keeping in line, of course, with our budget.

introductions turn out to be temporary guests on the supermarket shelves, their stay rarely exceeding a short 'test period', after which they disappear into oblivion.

On some occasions the cosmetic innovations can work, though success is almost always temporary. The consumer actually enjoys the variety of tastes and styles and consumption can increase, as in the case of Pickwick's varieties. However, because the respite is only temporary, the mere fact of the initial success might actually be damaging, since it might keep the company from perceiving the various dangers of getting involved in the cosmetic-innovation spiral.

The first danger is that producers too often focus on the *existing* market, which requires constantly increasing marketing and communication efforts. Whether the goal is to maintain or increase market share, the result is inevitably diminished returns, since the gains require disproportionate investments in communication. The producer perceives the 'market' with its current dimensions as a sort of set playing field, whether divided or not. Vision is blinkered. No thought is given to seeking out new, potential markets; imagination is stifled as companies concentrate on the narrow, technical task at hand.

Another danger is that the producer company begins to *believe* that the consumer views the cosmetic 'improvements' as seriously as it does. However, generally, what it might think of as an 'innovation' in the coffee market is simply another new flavour to the consumer. Such new varieties seldom lead to the securing of consumer preference and affection for the brand in the long run. This is all the more so if the company fritters away its communication plan in small sub-campaigns to support the different varieties, at the cost of a long-term marketing campaign.

Also, each new product variety requires ever-more detailed target-group profiles, but the question is whether the buyer the producer has in mind really exists. Put another way: one invents a target group after the fact, rather than the other way around. Companies come up with the product first and *then* wonder about the target group.

The producing company's orientation also tends to be overly governed by anything the R&D lab can come up with in the way of 'new' products, whether or not at the behest of the marketing department, whose innovation requests are increasingly taken from the competition. The wishes of the outside world, of the consumers themselves, do not play much of a role. The organisation becomes steadily more inward looking and increasingly ignores changes and trends in the society around it. When things go wrong, accusatory fingers are quickly pointed at the world outside. Failures are blamed on an unpredictable or uncooperative environment: currency fluctuations, 'the Japanese', a concurrent introduction by the competition, the competition's better product, the poor advertising campaign, or even uncooperative retailers.

The last danger is that the company's strategy becomes *competition* rather than *consumer* driven. Competitors are watched far too obsessively and taken too seriously – competitors that are probably all the while just as clueless as to how to proceed. Whenever a competitor happens to come up with a (cosmetic) improvement, panic breaks out for fear that the consumers will abandon the company's ship *en masse*. The R&D department is hastily instructed to 'go one better' or, at the very least, create an own version of the cosmetic innovation.

Whatever the specific dangers, they often – depending on the sector and the phase its products are in – amount to one thing: the company's returns from its cosmetic innovations begin to shrink. Even product-category leaders – e.g. in nappies, sanitary towels or detergents – have nothing but shrinking margins to show for their exhausting cosmetic-changes-based battles.

This sad reality is sometimes recognised by the players. For example, in a Dutch food retail magazine in 1996, the marketing heads of the detergent giants Unilever, Procter & Gamble, Henkel and Kortman Intradal publicly admitted for the first time that their extremely costly turf wars had escalated too much.

The reference to the detergent markets reveals one important variable which will determine how long such market battles will remain worthwhile for the companies involved. That variable is market saturation. If the companies are battling over saturated markets, they will both be defeated: margins will shrink fast. Women are not going to increase their sanitary towel consumption as a result of the war between Always and Libresse. If, on the other hand, there are prospects of market growth, such struggles can be extremely beneficial to all. This is the case, for example, in many newly opened markets where Coca-Cola and Pepsi have fought it out with their heavy-duty campaigns. Another more current example of 'mutual profiting' is found in the mobile telecommunications market, where all players benefit from each others' efforts to extend the market.

In the worst case, cosmetic innovations not only lead to poor margins, they can actually backfire and create consumer animosity. At a time when the consumers are becoming more discriminating and savvy, such innovations may make them respond cynically or even aggressively with regard to a particular product and its advertised benefits. Aware that, despite all the campaign promises, most products in this phase of the life cycle hardly differ from each other in terms of actual performance, consumers might begin disregarding new cosmetic innovations since they *do not meet real consumer needs*. Consumer groups might start expressing their growing irritation at the manner in which the products are advertised. Under such circumstances, the remote control serves as a handy tool to avoid confrontation and displeasure. The next natural step is for consumers to zap these brands off their shopping lists themselves. Companies should be careful and not allow themselves to get stuck in this phase – they have to recognise the need to move on to other approaches.

In conclusion, the distinguishing feature of the cosmetic innovation stage is that it is completely divorced from any real consumer needs.

Chapter 4

Bringing a Concept Brand to the Market

We have seen how the first three product-development phases can eventually lead to a low-margin dead end. The way out of this situation is to be found in embarking on a fourth, concepting, phase. New product development is replaced by new concept development – NCD instead of NPD, if you will. Business organisation also begins to change, as companies become communication or concept oriented. We will see that concepting is the step that follows positioning and repositioning in the evolution of marketing.

4.1   Concepting: phase four in product development

In the third, marketing-oriented phase, the idea of 'brand thinking' begins to take root, and brand development and expansion become important corporate objectives. However, these efforts are primarily directed at existing brands, which originate in traditional production processes or company names. In other words, *existing* brands provide the raw material for the new ones.

Concept brands differ from classic 'product brands' in that they do not claim any intrinsic qualities, improvements (genuine or cosmetic) or added values. Instead, as we have seen, they offer visions, attitudes, convictions, motivations and 'wavelengths' of various sorts. The particular concept provides the governing

guidelines for the brand's development and means of implementation – from the tone of communication and style, to product
varieties, pricing and distribution.

Communication – which encompasses all aspects of the brand's
behaviour – is the most important of these means. It articulates
the meaning behind the concept brand; it gives the concept
substance. The manner of communicating the concept is very
precisely determined and carefully protected from the concept's
inception. This includes, for instance, the kinds of emotion and
behaviour elicited – that is, the brand's 'codes'; how the brand is
to react to current events; what the brand sponsor wants and does
not want; how the concept is to be manifested and how
frequently.

The most difficult feature of concepting is that it deals with
emotions and *feelings*. For this reason, many companies find that
the management task is more complicated than it is for a concrete
product. When these factors are successfully managed, however,
the payoff to companies can be enormous: namely, concept
brands that are completely original and practically inimitable.
This is the secret to their relative impregnability and durability.

While concrete products seem to offer companies security, we
have seen that from the early product-development stages
onwards, this is not really so. Imitation by the competition is
relatively easy, so that establishing a clear lead over other
companies is impossible. In contrast, emotions and feelings
associated with a concept brand may, at first sight, seem to be
very tenuous, but they are actually far more secure and durable
than many a product improvement. This is because a personal
world built up by the consumer in response to a concept is much
more difficult for competitors to replicate. Getting a handle on all
the codes underlying a competitor's concept brand is next to
impossible. Compare this with the relatively simple task of
studying and quickly copying a new dryness layer in a sanitary
towel or airbags in automobiles. Besides, and just as important,
consumers will regard companies that attempt to reproduce a
competitor's concept as pathetic, unimaginative 'copycats', and
will reject them as such – it is one thing to copy a product, and
quite another to copy a concept.

Let us take the durability of McDonald's concept, for example. Making hamburgers is no great secret; indeed, many, such as Burger King, arguably make better ones than the company with the golden arches. However, the McDonald's concept – that is, the 'McDonald's feeling' – has remained practically impregnable to imitators for years.

Benetton is another good example. With its origins in a small-scale production company, it was able to formulate a concept for the brand, which has firmly established it in today's market. The 'United Colors of Benetton' is a (particular) cosmopolitan vision of the world. A vision that expresses the idea that young people the world over are part of one big, open-minded, joyful family. It creates one unified, colourful world out of differences in colour and race: 'If you believe all young people of the world are one family, then join us. Join Benetton'.

This, of course, is *my* interpretation of Benetton's concept. Each of us can interpret it as he or she sees fit: the 'creators' would not be able to help us out, since they themselves in all likelihood originally only had a vague sense of the path they should take. Well, this vague sense resulted in a worldwide network of 7000 stores in 120 countries!

Benetton's success is therefore not due to the quality of its materials, workmanship or particular fashion statement – the conventional paths to success in the clothing world. Its success is based on a strong and consistent concept. Early on, Benetton opted for a particular concept, a very personal image, and stuck to it. Benetton does not flow with the currents of fashion. In setting the lines for the brand's behaviour, the company made some perceptive choices in order to underpin its philosophy. For example, Benetton's colour scheme, though relatively limited, reflects the extreme colourfulness of the world: one can buy a single sweater model in eight different colours. This way, one can have one's own colour while having a relationship with the owner of the same sweater, but of another colour. The scheme, in line with the Benetton concept, thus provides the consumer with the possibility of expressing both individuality and solidarity.

Benetton's distribution network has also been built up in line with its concept. The initial focus was on locations where the multicultural, increasingly internationally oriented following is most often found: in the larger cities. Later, it was extended to smaller centres, which could never have been the initial locations for the Benetton's cosmopolitanism. Today, Benetton stores are found all over the world in centres both large and small. In another example of consistent brand behaviour, the company's magazine, *Colors*, brings elements of the Benetton concept field, using another medium, to its following worldwide.

The durability of the Benetton concept is beyond dispute. Its communications – with one controversial exception we will deal with later – have remained faithful to and consistent with the original concept. Its products, in contrast, have not needed to have these features over time. In fact, as in the case of the best concepts, its importance – the importance of the Benetton world – far outstrips that of its products.

Has any company succeeded in copying the Benetton concept? Has any company built up the same type of network with the same concept? The answer to both questions in my view is clearly no. Furthermore, one senses that even if there were such an imitator, the consumers would not have gone near its stores, because, as mentioned earlier, *consumers perceive concept copiers as cheap and second-rate*. From this it can be inferred that a distinguishing characteristic of concept brands is that they are, by definition, unique and original. Put another way: Would an imitation Madonna or Bette Midler attract any fans?

What a contrast to how consumers respond to companies that copy features of 'tangible' products! There is nothing wrong with that: it is seen as logical, even responsible, behaviour; an effort to provide them with state-of-the-art technology, often at a lower price. Indeed, consumers seem to demand that competing products be similar; that they all meet the same minimum standards.

Some brands have been in this fourth, concepting phase of product development for a number of years, while others have arisen over the course of the last decade. Here is a sampling of the old and new: Apple, Ben & Jerry's, Calvin Klein, Caterpillar, Club Med, CNN, Davidoff, Diesel, the Discovery Channel, Eurocamp, Ikea, Marlboro, MTV, Planet Hollywood, Peter Stuyvesant, The Body Shop, Sanex, Smart Car and Swatch.

The distinguishing feature of all concept brands is their uniqueness and originality – prior to their introduction no following had evolved around such a concept.

4.2 Concepting: beyond positioning

We have seen how product development within corporations evolves until a situation is reached in which further innovation no longer makes economic sense. Some companies nevertheless hopefully persist with the cosmetic improvements. Other companies rely more on changes in their marketing and communications than on actually modifying products themselves, if only cosmetically. In other words, they turn to *positioning*: the addition of *expressive* values to the product to give it a lease on market life.

Not surprisingly, positioning occurs first in so-called 'fast-moving consumer goods', precisely because the options for cosmetic improvements in these products are limited and quickly used up. Producers of beer, soft drinks, cigarettes, detergents, shampoos and breakfast cereals, for example, realise that the intrinsic value of their products is no longer distinctive or important enough to win or maintain the consumer's favour. They thus began using communication to add expressive value to the product, shifting attention from the product to the *brand*, imbued with an emotional charge and a 'personality'.

Pepsi positions itself as the 'next generation' cola; Budweiser as the 'king of beers', and Silk Cut as the low-tar cigarette. However, positioning is not confined to the fast-movers. Luxury products also position themselves, above and beyond the status value they have already attained: Samsonite becomes the most durable travel companion; Volvo is identified with safety; and Jack Daniels becomes the carefully crafted whisky that always remains true to its origins.

The attempt to occupy a distinctive 'position in the consumer's mind' through positioning has been very fruitful for a great number of companies. This is particularly true of the strong market players that have the courage to take the initiative and stick to it. Imitators sprout up and try to claim the same position in their communications, but they have a hard time dislodging well-positioned brands. Their attempts, if anything, only succeed in confusing the consumer.

The various waves of positioning and repositioning have resulted in the slow crystallisation of many saturated markets. Typically, a small number of players, having built strong brands, manage to hold on to their positions, while others are forced to limit themselves to less attractive options, like concentrating on cheaper, B brands or even producing for third parties. These are the losers in the battle for a position in the consumer's mind.

It should be clear that in its focus on communication and on winning over the consumer's mind, positioning is a precursor to concepting. However, even if concepting is the next natural step from positioning, it is important to bear in mind three key differences between the two:

(1) Positioning is based on communicating added values, concepting on concepts.
(2) Positioning relies on a brand's surface, concepting on a brand's 'soul'.
(3) Positioning is guided by specific, existing markets, concepting by a wide range of existing and still-to-be-created markets.

Positioning is the communication of *added values*. A company already has a particular product or service, and only when market saturation begins to threaten does it resort, through positioning, to adding a particular distinctive expressive feature and trying to occupy a particular mental position. Concepting, in contrast, brings a concept, such as a philosophy, an attitude, a value system or a mentality to the market. The concept provides the field, or the fertile ground, for subsequent product introductions. Under concepting, products can be removed as easily as they can be introduced. The Virgin concept, for example, has an extremely broad field of product possibilities, all of which, from airlines to colas, from radio to railroad services, and from insurances to vodkas, radiate the concept's meaning. However, the Virgin concept is not dependent on any one product or product group: it has an autonomous life.

Since the intrinsic nature of a product is the same as that of the competition, positioning often amounts to adding a veneer, or a layer of make-up, which is applied in a slightly different way from that of the competition. This veneer is simply *thought up*: it is not rooted in the company's or the brand's history. Concepting, in contrast, is dedicated to radiating the 'soul' of the brand: it is a depth phenomenon, and it is unchanging and unchangeable. Although Ikea's or Davidoff's product selection might change, as the companies adapt to changing contemporary images and the wishes of the consumer, the 'soul' of the Ikea and Davidoff concepts remains unchanged.

Positioning is resorted to within *existing, saturated* markets. The producing company attempts to distinguish itself from the competition by means of its own communication territory, and the existing consumers are, as it were, divided by the different players. Concepting, on the other hand, uses the concept to attract followers from *all kinds of markets, current and future.* The strength of the concept itself and the ensuing variety of products brought to the market create a unique field of influence which transcends all sorts of markets and cannot be categorised as any single type of market.

Despite these differences, it is clear that positioning is the forerunner of concepting: the strongest feature they have in common is the perception that distinct values are more important than distinct product features. This is reflected in the fact that the brand marketing mix under positioning involves a great deal of communication. However, under concepting, of course,

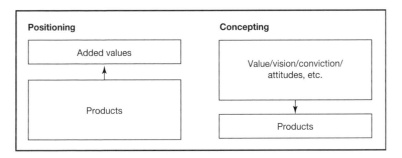

Figure 4.1 In concepting, products are secondary.

communication takes on an even greater, central significance, while products become even less important than they are under positioning.

The relative importance of the concept and the product can be seen in the example of three concept brands: Boss, Nike and Ikea. People who buy Boss socks do so because they have the Boss brand. They take for granted that their favourite brand will offer good product quality. Similarly, nobody doubts the quality of Nike shoes. The consumers buy them because they identify with Nike's philosophy and want to wear anything that has the 'swoosh' logo on it. An Ikea bookcase of mediocre quality but fashionable design – the kind that will only last for three years – will be bought because it is an Ikea product; because Ikea represents a vision that challenges the idea that you have to stick to the same oak furniture from your wedding day to your diamond anniversary. In other words, the furniture is of great quality for a product that is expected to last three years! Ikea, in this case, represents the idea that you are free to change the furnishings of your home as often as you choose. That is part of the concept that you buy into.

Chapter 5

From Target Groups to Following

Concepting involves a completely different perception of consumers and the process of their grouping. We have already seen that under this approach the particular concept is created first and the consumer groups – the brand's following – is elicited subsequently. The notion of a target group no longer applies. The company does not – along with its competitors – aim at clearly defined sociodemographic or purchasing-behaviour groups.

Before examining the notion of a following under concepting, let us first look at how target groups have been defined historically and the main drawbacks of the approach.

5.1 Target-group drawbacks

The first potential problem with group targeting is that of *myth-making*. Marketing and communication professionals tend initially to define target groups in a precise fashion, using two-dimensional criteria such as age, sex, place of residence, income, purchasing- and use-behaviour and so on. Later, when markets become saturated and the turf battle becomes fiercer, they often begin to fine-tune their definitions, making them more and more subtle. In the process, they can also make them more and more unreal and mythical. The typical target group definition implicit in many half- or full-page ads of quality magazines, pictures a consumer who is so idealised, one wonders whether she or he exists – or indeed can *ever* exist – at all. The target group is thus often refined out of existence, though the advertising agencies fervently believe in and urge their clients to pursue them.

The second potential problem with the target group approach is that, given market saturation and the large number of producers, companies end up with *indistinguishable target-group images*, rendering any brand differentiation virtually impossible. Over the past few years, advertising agencies have made use of so-called 'mood boards' when fine-tuning their target-group definitions. A vast improvement over dry definition parameters like 'urban housewives aged 25–40', the mood boards give copy-writers a much clearer idea of the group to which the message is to be targeted: the potential consumer is personalised and the right tone is easier to strike. The problem is that however good their mood boards, companies producing the same product end up targeting the same groups. What is the difference, for example, between the Visa and the MasterCard, or the Ford and the Opel, or the Heineken and the Budweiser, or the Compaq and Macintosh target groups? Is there such a thing as a mortgage broker who *does not* market to 'young families' as a target group? In short, when markets are saturated and cluttered with producers, group targeting offers no way out.

The target-group approach also often results in *brand strait-jacketing*. This is a product of the company's sticking too closely to so-called buyer profiles. For example, let us assume that research indicates that the existing buyer group for a particular whisky brand can be described as 'male, aged 42, living in the metropolitan area, a *New York Times* reader and probably a BMW rather than a Mercedes driver'. Many companies make the mistake of using such a profile to define their target group, even before the brand's marketing and communication activities have been fully developed. The brand is thus prematurely strait-jacketed; its development is stifled; and other consumer groups are excluded.

A counterpart to the strait-jacketing problem is that of *brand stereotyping*, which can result from group targeting. In this case, the communication to the target group is done in such a way that brand becomes, in the public's eye, completely identified with the specific target group. The brand therefore gets locked in with a particular stereotype, with the effect that other potential consumers keep away because they do not want to be lumped in with that stereotype – the Volvo or Saab identification with 'yuppies' is a case in point, as is Fanta's with children.

From the perspective of marketing or positioning handbooks, the agency has done a fantastic job in such cases: the target group has been captured; the mission accomplished. Now it is simply a matter of using communications to cultivate or confirm existing users. Problems arise, however, when the client demands further growth from the brand. The agencies desperately try to formulate ways of attracting new buyers without alienating the old. More often than not this is impossible. Indeed, most companies end up having to come to terms with the brand's limitations. This was the case of *Het Parool*, a major Dutch newspaper, which struggled for years in an attempt to broaden its appeal beyond its initial target group of Amsterdammers: to no avail. PCM, the parent company, finally gave up and decided to reach other groups with new publications.

While PCM was thus forced to accept these growth limitations, others have done so willingly, from the beginning. Indeed, solving the problem by developing new brands to cater for the excluded groups is not that uncommon. It is known as the 'Unilever model' of broad brand portfolio development; named after the company that has, for example, a portfolio of butter brands – Blue Band, Becel, Effi, Promise, Country Crock, Flora, Rama and Latta – which effectively covers the whole range of potential consumers. Though this option is of course only open to the very large companies, smaller ones can gain some of the benefits of portfolio extension by means of mergers – recent examples can be found in the Martini/Bacardi, Heineken/Amstel, Daimler/Chrysler, NationsBank/BankAmerica, BP/Mobil and Worldcom/MCI cases.

5.2 Eliciting a following

The definition of a concept's following is really quite simple: all those who relate to or identify with the brand's concept – e.g. an attitude, mentality or 'world'. Before a following can be elicited, however, a concepting team must be in place and have its fingers on the pulse of society, registering ongoing changes and tendencies in its beat.

Anticipating developments, the team identifies and develops the concept to be subsequently embodied in products. While it may be that the team sees the new concept as being of more interest to one group than another, the team will not become group-fixated, as it were. It will not feel obliged to provide a highly detailed description of groups, since its conviction is that there is the potential for the emergence of a following, that is, of a wide variety of people participating in the same concept. When referring to potential consumers, the team is most likely to say things like: 'We know for certain that there is a growing group of people who feel at home with..., who are attracted to..., who are sick of..., who are searching for..., who simply like our idea', and so on.

Although such words seem vague, they are anything but. They refer to real people scattered throughout society (and all over the globe); such as the millions on our planet who believe we should perceive the world as a big family – the essence of Benetton's concept. Or the many who believe TV should go beyond inane soap operas and quiz shows, as reflected in Discovery Channel's vision. In this 'post-materialistic' age, followings such as these are more likely to offer opportunities than do traditionally defined target groups.

Concepting does not actually challenge the basic principle of marketing: namely, listening to what the market wants. The difference today is that the market's demands are not focused on concrete objects or products; instead, they reflect *mental* needs.[1] This takes a little getting used to for marketing people, but such mental needs clearly exist, and many brands are successfully meeting them: for example, the need to identify with non-conformism and anti-establishmentarianism (Virgin's concept), animal friendliness (The Body Shop's) or social consciousness (Ben & Jerry's).

---

1. See Evolution of Entrepreneurship table on page 115.

Although we have noted that a following can cut across all sociodemographic groups, it is also true that it tends to start out as a small fan club, or core group. At first, a core group arises in response to the concept newly brought onto the market. Indeed, the concepting team's first objective after having defined the concept itself is to promote the emergence of such a *core group*. It could even be said that, at this stage, they are in the business of creating a following, more than a product itself.

Look at the following Ikea managed to create. Before the company appeared, market research had never identified a target group of 'casual buyers of pick-it-up-yourself and assemble-it-at-home furniture'. Neither was there a target group of 'fans of Scandinavian furnishing styles'. Ikea's eventual customers, that enormous following, which initially put up with parking on soggy fields, the disappointment of stock-outs and the long line-ups, and finding that the goods they came for had been sold out, were elicited and nurtured by the Ikea concept itself. For this reason it is practically impossible for other companies to lure customers away from the Swedish furniture giant.

The notion of a following effectively avoids the strait-jacketing problems we discussed earlier with the use of group targeting. Everybody is welcome to join a concept following. You will never hear a concepting-team member using exclusionary language: 'Yes, but those people don't fit in with our target group'. This amounts to throwing business away. Concepting is open and inviting to all: 'Anyone who feels they can relate to our vision is more than welcome'. This is why, for example, Nike's following no longer consists exclusively of runners, its original core group, but encompasses everyone who embraces the notion of persistence, self-confidence, aspiration and performance as important in life. Nike's concept can touch everyone, from the top athlete, to the middle-aged heart-rehabilitation patient, to the physically handicapped. The other problem encountered by the target-group approach, namely, of the predetermined and unchanging dimension of the group, is also irrelevant under concepting. In fact, the following should actually be perceived as continuously growing. If the concept is well conceived and implemented, its core group will take it into their living environments, where it will attract new followers. The target group is never delineated, and estimates of potential sales volume cannot be drawn up as in traditional marketing.

In fact, the most that can be done under concepting is to measure *ex post* the number and type of customers that have joined the following. Let us look at the Ikea case again. When it began operations in the European market in the 1970s, it offered young families 'young', inexpensive, predominantly wooden furniture and small decorative furnishings. Naturally, the families occasionally took their parents along with them to the store, in this way expanding Ikea's following. Today, 20 years later, the young families are in their 40s, and their parents in their 60s. Ikea has kept up with them, and now offers its concept to a huge, trans-generational following. While the company's selection has grown along with the more diversified tastes in the expanding following, the Ikea concept has not budged an inch. Started in Sweden in 1948, today Ikea has more than 159 stores in 30 countries with 61,700 employees, and the concept is still winning converts. This unpredictability of the ultimate following is one of concepting's characteristics: how far the concentric circles will travel away from the core group is always an open question.

Chapter 6
Coming Up with Concepts

Concepting ideas are born in people's minds: in your own mind, in the mind of others or as a result of your minds working together. The main condition is that you be open to those unsought flashes that emerge in an unstructured, creative-thinking process, the fruitfulness of which depends on openness and sensitivity to the outside world. Good conceptual ideas stem more from intuitive 'feelings' than from hard analysis or extrapolations of market facts and figures.

Let us look at some examples of how concepts have been developed, before presenting a ten-step programme for setting up a concepting process from scratch and examining possible means of using concepts developed by others.

6.1   A keen interest in people

Whether it is done alone or in a team, creating new concepts is not an academic or even a brainstorming exercise. I believe brainstorming can be a helpful tool for solving a number of problems, but it is not the appropriate means for creating good concept brands. Its boundaries tend to be too restrictive: the process too physically constrained, intellectual and distant from the consumer.

Good concepting requires close involvement in the social environment. The best method available is to step into the living spaces of people and to experience their lives along with them.

Only by getting under their skin in this way is it possible to discover what moves, drives, annoys or pleases them: how and why they behave as individuals or as a group. This is the stuff of good concepting.

Steve Jobs knows this. The founder of Apple noticed how people at work wrestled with their computers. They perceived the machines more as extensions of administrative processes than of themselves. He observed how people, often reluctantly, used the large and awkward things merely as glorified typewriters with memories and correction keys. His vision for Apple emerged from these observations: if management wanted to increase employee productivity, it needed computers that were 'fun', 'friendly' and accessible to everyone. Only then would people use them with pleasure, excite others about them and thereby increase productivity.

This was the starting point for the Apple concept. It led to the development of user-friendly, accessible software and a light-weight portable casing – which, incidentally, made the process of 'spreading the word' by the core group easier. It also laid the basis for the tone of Apple's communications – directed at the user rather than at management – and paved the way for the company's jovial, unconventional logo and advertising. In line with its concentration on users and people, Apple spared no effort to avoid the 'business-to-business' image its competitors projected. This image inevitably portrayed them as conventional and old-fashioned; as producers of systems for command-and-control hierarchical organisations.

The Apple concept demonstrates a particularly important feature of concepting that we touched on earlier – namely, that the tangible product takes a back seat to the intangible one, i.e. the concept. Clearly, engineers alone would never have hit on the Apple concept had they been asked to develop 'the next generation of computers': they would probably have proposed a heavier IBM-like clone.

The Diesel concept is another case in point. The fashion brand's creator, Renzo Rosso, has built his concept upon the perception that young people are less and less willing to accept fashion dictated from on high. He came to this conclusion after travelling and speaking at length with them. Diesel's concept, in a nutshell, is something like: 'We don't impose a particular style on you: you determine your own style by mixing together and creating your *own* individual world with the multifarious Diesel brand products'.

Furthermore, Diesel's products never stagnate. Rosso does not believe in hiring a chief designer, since he or she would tend to develop a particular style which might land Diesel in a rut. Instead, every year he brings together a new team of young designers whom he then sends out to all corners of the world to mingle with young people: in discos, clubs, bars and shopping centres. The designers then go to work producing a collection of approximately 10,000 items. Unsurprisingly, the collection includes a mix of completely clashing styles. However, that is what makes the concept fun (and effective): customers can put together their very own personal mixes, however bizarre and wacky. A panther-print T-shirt, herring-bone striped pants and tangerine-orange shoes: 'That's me!'

Diesel's unique approach to communication reflects its concept perfectly. The ads are not so much concerned with presenting the clothing – which is not even pictured in a flattering way – as they are with presenting an ironic, absurdist philosophy of life. Indeed, they are often targeted at undermining advertising itself. They give advertising clichés the wry treatment, portraying winners who seem to be losers, and showing impossible, often disagreeable situations. Diesel's ironic payoff reads: 'Diesel: For successful living'.

Let us look at another example: Eurocamp, the camping resort organisation. Those who thought up the Eurocamp concept were no tent makers or traditional tour operators. They were simply people who realised that individuals accustomed to the joys of travelling, going out and the freedom afforded by a double-income standard of living had big problems foregoing these pleasures when settling down and having children. Although they were aware that campgrounds offered a traditional solution, a place where children could always quickly make friends and parents could get some much-needed rest, they disliked their middle-class image – not to speak of the prospect of the packed car or caravan and the unwieldy camping equipment.

What Eurocamp has done is give camping a new *meaning*. It set up large, completely furnished and equipped tents – mattressed beds, refrigerators, etc. – on spacious sites on small, good-quality campgrounds. Eurocamp animators welcome the families and remain at their disposal for their entire stay, organising activities for the children so that parents can have a few hours to themselves and rediscover just how romantic a tent can be!

The minute you make your booking you become part of the Eurocamp family. A few months before going on your camping vacation, your family receives regular information about the campground it is to visit: family members can start enjoying the prospect of the vacation long before they arrive. Upon your return home, of course, you are given the opportunity to express your honest opinion of your Eurocamp stay and offer suggestions for improvements. You are given a strong sense, throughout, that you belong to a valued group. Indeed, Eurocamp communicates more directly with its following than any other travel company. Have you, as a consumer, ever had any contact with any representative of a big tour operator, except perhaps when making a complaint?

Eurocamp's concept does not involve merely renting campsites or guaranteeing a reservation: it involves personal attention and a unique vacation experience which, incidentally, also contains an extra, subtle status ingredient. Eurocamp has grown to attract a large following, many of whom make repeat bookings long before the traditional reservation season.

Could any of these three concepting examples have originated from traditional market studies and consumer research? I think not.

6.2 Concepters

Much like the joyful 'Eureka!' cry of the inventor in his garden shed, those individuals who hit on concept ideas – the *concepters* – are overcome with the joyful sensation of having come up with a great idea. They have a special sense for something, devote all their energy to it and succeed. This is an experience shared by all great concepters like Steve Jobs (Apple), Richard Branson (Virgin), Ingvar Kamprad (Ikea), Eckard Wintzen (BSO), Annita Roddick (The Body Shop) and many of the up-and-coming figures.

The intricacies of how someone comes up with a concept after 'sensing' and thinking through future scenarios and intuiting which direction things will take are undoubtedly a secret deeply nestled in the brain. It is possible, however, to sketch a profile of the kind of people who are likely to become successful concepters.

To begin with, they tend to be the kind of people who are constantly curious and wondering about everything. With extremely widespread interests, they favour multi-disciplinary and generalist attitudes. These qualities render the process of making connections – conscious or unconscious – between their multi-faceted experiences much easier than it is for others. They dare to give their intuition free rein, shrugging off criticism of those who disapprove of this human faculty for being too vague. Deep down they know and feel that the product of their intuition reflects the experience of both their reason and their emotion – it is rooted in both hemispheres of their brain. They are also comfortable with uncertainty; indeed, they often seek it out as a source of challenges. 'Impossible' is not part of their vocabulary. Lastly, they are very sensitive to currents and tendencies. Their interest in history gives them a better grasp of developments and clearer insights into the future. They have a bird's-eye view on people and society – some would call this 'vision'.

Concepters are not the sort of people who are purposefully and consciously preoccupied with coming up with the new ideas: 'Now I'm going to sit down and think up a brand-new concept!' Rather, their ideas usually surface suddenly, of their own accord, as a spontaneous result of their continual interest in the surrounding world. I have noticed that they always carry around a number of concepts 'in their heads', even while they are in the process of successfully implementing one in particular. (They often bemoan this situation, since by concentrating on the implementation of one, they cannot dedicate the time they would like to to others.)

The other key talent concepters are blessed with is the ability to convince – nay, excite – others about their ideas. This is particularly difficult under concepting because the ideas are very abstract and mental, as it were. Getting people excited about a concrete idea, such as a light-bulb, is naturally far easier than doing so for a concept. Successful concepters are therefore good communicators: they listen well and they are good at getting their ideas across. Thanks to this skill, they are good at inspiring confidence and enthusiasm in others.

However, these paragons do have their weaknesses, of course. The one I have observed most often is their tendency to have below-par organisational skills. Whether because they do not have the capability or simply choose not to exercise it, it seems concepters are more in their element dealing with the artistic or even the spiritual side of things – in developing and implementing the concept. For this reason, companies need more than concepters in their concepting teams. They need complementary capabilities, such as organisational and administrative skills – this is particularly the case in concept implementation.

6.3   Ten steps to a concepting team

If you, as a company manager, decide to establish a team to come up with new concepts, you must first ask yourself whether you have the necessary talented people in-house. If so, then remember that they need the time and space to do the concepting work. In *Competing for the Future*,[1] Hamel and Prahalad mention studies showing that managers themselves only spend a few minutes a day thinking about and developing ideas for the future. Busy with the here and now, with keeping competition at bay, they have little time for such activities. One can expect that the rest of the organisation is also directed at dealing with daily problems, most probably within the context of the prevailing rules, production methods, behavioural codes and corporate culture in general.

Unsurprisingly, such a context is not at all appropriate to concepting. We have seen that concepting requires an atmosphere of freedom, and that concepters are people whose skills require

1.   G. Hamel and C.K. Prahalad (1994) *Competing for the Future*. Boston: Harvard Business School.

open and unfettered environments in which to bloom. They cannot be subject to corporate organisation and culture while they 'inhale' society's trends and developments, and become absorbed in the world of human behaviour. For this reason, concepting cannot be assigned to a work group, the members of which spend a few hours a week thinking up concepts and the rest of the time taking care of regular business.

The general principles to keep in mind therefore are that concepting requires complete immersion, dedication and ample time. Specifically, I would suggest the following ten steps in the establishment of a concepting team:

(1) Find one or two *talented employees* who seem to fit the concepting character sketch we have talked about above. These potential concepters often have the tell-tale characteristic of being know-it-all types. They are usually considered to be too creative; they tend to claim they could improve things and often dare to express (constructive) criticism about what is going on in the company. Often finding their ambitions constrained by the prevailing corporate culture, they frequently express their intention to seek their fortune elsewhere (in fact, companies often let such valuable resources slip away). These people should form the core of your concepting team. Allow them to dedicate 100% of their time to the task and relieve them of any and all other responsibilities, and have them report directly to the most visionary members of the management team.

(2) Define your concepting team's *mission*, although this should not be too detailed. Try something like this: 'Create new concepts, whose behaviour – i.e. name, logo and communication – represents a particular mentality, attitude, philosophy, etc., which has the potential to create a strong following'.

(3) Provide the team with its *own space*. It should be located off-site, away from the existing corporate facilities. Use your imagination; for example, rent them space above a bar in the city centre.

(4) Allow the concepting team *complete freedom* to do its work, but do not let them float their initial ideas by their former colleagues in the parent organisation, be they in production, sales or marketing: these will inevitably respond negatively. Unable to distance themselves from their traditional perspectives, their reactions will be predictable: 'It doesn't fit into the current product line'; 'There's no market for it'; 'It's logistically impossible'; 'We have different distribution channels'; 'It's not our line of business'; and so on.

(5) Allocate the team a *generous budget* and give them *carte blanche* within it. Do not be surprised, for example, if they suddenly fly off to Barcelona, Los Angeles or Seattle for inspiration. Also do not be surprised by the number of magazines they subscribe to, or the pile of literature they buy or the time they spend surfing the internet. Judge them only by the concepts they come up with, not by how they come up with them.

(6) Allow the team to contract *independent resources* to complement their skills with outside talent, whether or not attached to specialised, concepting agencies. They must have the freedom to incorporate specialists of all sorts – for any period of time – to participate and give the process a fresh boost or provide good sounding boards for raw ideas. These people might include entrepreneurs, trend watchers, designers and communication 'animals' – not, of course, communications theorists. In their selection, the team should be aware that the excellence of the person's *professional* skills is not decisive. That is, they need not be the best designers or the best TV commercial producers. However, they do need to be extremely talented at looking beyond their own fields, and identifying its interconnections with the outside world. Be careful not to build a concepting team of more than five or six members.

(7) Give the concepting team nine months to produce a selection of five to ten testable concepts. Encourage them also to save

ideas that seem interesting, but that do not quite meet their mission, for possible future use. Remember, good concepts are very rare. Do not approve or reject any concept up-front. Organise *extensive concept testing* by people who might be potential followers. Have the entire concepting team observe every one of the testing sessions. The viability of concepts can only be ascertained in this manner, and not by leafing through research reports carried out by third parties after the tests are complete. You will learn nothing from 'checking the research'. Indeed, each and every consumer reaction during the testing itself might prove crucial to further refining the concept – it could even spark the birth of an entirely new one. Stick to the same (external) testing-session moderator and researchers: they too can become very useful as repositories of knowledge and experience related to the concepts.

(8) Once you have the handful of concepts that have passed through the testing process – your concept short-list – *present them to the rest of the management, before surprising the rest of the organisation.*

(9) Consider *other factors*, like production, distribution and resource allocation, only after you have your concepting short-list.

(10) *Maintain the momentum.* Remember that concepting is a process: it does not come to an end once the concept is launched. In fact, it is never over: the concept has to be nurtured with continuous interaction with consumers.

In sum, when you establish a concepting team you are building your own concept hot-house, in what is, in my view, a very interesting and affordable proposition for most companies. Ultimately, if successful, it should lead you to develop a fully fledged New Concept Development (NCD) section alongside the classic New Product Development (NPD).

6.4 Drawing on others' concepts

There is also, of course, always the possibility of drawing on someone else's concept. As noted above, there are plenty of people walking around with ideas in their heads, and many lack the resources to bring them to fruition. In most cases they have not yet succeeded in getting through to the right decision makers, despite incessantly knocking on their doors. Ask them to drop by and if you find they are on to a good thing, offer them the chance to form a concepting unit around it – it could lead to a very beneficial mutual undertaking.

Another option is to turn to the growing number of *concepting agencies*. Frequently spin-offs of communication agencies of various types, these agencies either develop their own concept brands, which they then sell to interested companies, or work on an assignment basis for clients. Of the outside entities, concepting agencies, given their specialisation, are in the best position to introduce, communicate and accompany a concept brand in the market.

Lastly, you could simply travel around searching for concepts that are working elsewhere and still have not been tried in your market. Though this is not the most imaginative course, what is wrong with introducing an effective concept if the proprietary company has no plans – or cannot afford – to expand beyond its own market? A company in this position is quite likely to welcome a buyer interested in implementing its concept elsewhere in the world, either on its own or in a joint venture.

Companies can even trade their successful concepts with each other. Assuming the concepts are easily integrated into the respective organisations, both companies can significantly strengthen their brand portfolios in this manner.

Chapter 7

Determining a Concept's Feasibility

Under classic product-development practices, a number of methods are used to determine whether or not a new product or product innovation stands a chance of succeeding in the market. The products are tested in the company laboratory in a variety of other ways to compare their performance with those of the competition. Sometimes, even new production test facilities are built in order to research production feasibility, often at very substantial cost. Products are also tested in home-usage tests, or group interviews of target-group members are carried out by marketing research companies. In most cases the tests cover both the product's performance and its packaging. Additional tests take place at retail outlets, but unfortunately, at this stage, if the consumers reject it, it is too late: the investment is down the drain.

Concepting takes a very different approach: by testing concepts instead of products and involving consumers and retailers, it minimises risk while extending durability.

7.1 Continuous consumer involvement

Since concepting begins with attitudes, experiences, philosophies and so on, and no products, the question is: How does one test such abstract notions? Could the Benetton feeling, or the need for a fast-food chain embodied by the McDonald's concept have been tested? How could one tell whether the 'world of Winfield' would work? Would Steve Jobs' Apple concept have received a positive evaluation in a buyer-research study, at a time when computerisation was seen as a means of conserving corporate hierarchies?

One thing is certain: classic research methodology conducted *at the end of a product-development process does not work*; even in the best of circumstances its results are dubious. As we saw in the previous chapter's ten steps, under concepting, interaction with consumers is an integral part of the process from the start, long before products have been considered. Actually, one could almost say that the consumer is a fully fledged member of the concepting team throughout the whole life of a concept – from its very conception.

The consumer's participation is implicit at the time the concepting-team members are chosen. Openness and very sensitive antennae to the behaviour of others, as we have seen, are key criteria in the team's selection of internal people and, particularly, of those outside the organisation, such as entrepreneurs, designers and creatives. These people do not live in ivory towers. They are 'out on the street', consuming and living along with the consumers: eyes always open, watching and 'sensing'. They are in a privileged and unique position to discover just the kind of concept that is likely to have strong appeal.

Concepts arising out of this process tend therefore to be solidly based on real – though abstract – consumer needs. When a concept brand responding to these needs is introduced, it stands a very good chance of succeeding. Compare this with classic product development, which entails technicians and marketing people shut up behind company walls, thinking up (cosmetic) innovations in the hope that they might appeal to the consumer.

Concepting involves making manifold contacts with consumers during the early phase of the concepting process. Once the team, after a few months, has come up with some concept ideas, these are then presented to consumers using small focus groups – step 7 in the process discussed in the previous chapter. This does not involve elaborately produced test products and packaging, but a broad sampling of (rough) items that could fit into the new brand's world. The brand image – a roughly sketched combination of the brand's textual and visual elements, and its logo or badge – is applied to a variety of objects, for instance, T-shirts, store fronts and CD sleeves.

During this process, the team also tests a draft concept statement and concept boards, videos, music, etc., portraying the world of the concept. In a constant, interactive process, the potential followers provide their spontaneous reaction and the concept is slowly perfected. If their reactions clash with the envisaged concept, the process is aborted: the concept is not a good one. However, such ideas are not thrown away. Concepting's logic is non-linear: since teams 'feel' their way to concepts, the failure of one concept often provides the key to the later development of another, successful one.

What this consumer interaction amounts to is not a nervous observation behind one-way mirrors, in the hope that the consumers will erupt in unbridled enthusiasm at the sight of the developers' new 'baby'. It is about presenting them with a number of roughly developed brands and carefully *watching* and *listening* to their reactions; these provide the raw material for the next round of exercises. A number of such sessions are carried out over the course of a few months. Slowly, a clear picture emerges of those concepts that have the best chance of succeeding.

Naturally, this process can be tough on the concepting team. Creatives, for example, who have spent hours and hours honing their designs or logos, are apt to start pulling their hair out as they watch consumers nonchalantly brush their masterpieces aside – consumers are (fortunately) brutally honest in this type of research. Even the more business-oriented members of the team can often be heard cursing under their breath, when it becomes obvious that they still have a long road ahead of them. Psychologically, the trick is for members not to attach themselves too much to their ideas – to see them as first inputs in the process and to use the consumer reactions as the catalysts for better ideas.

The team members thus should follow and be continuously involved in the research – a misleadingly cold term for a process that is a dynamic and exciting experience: perhaps 'discovery session' would be more accurate. Such involvement should give them deep insight into the consumer's interaction with the concept and into where it should be taken. At times the teams improvise and modify the concept on the spot, seeking the consumer's reaction. Needless to say, concepting-team members who confidently announce that they would prefer not to be involved and want to wait and see what the research report has to say, do not belong: distant non-involvement and consumer sensitivity are incompatible.

Since the test moderators and researchers in the course of their work also accumulate knowledge about consumer attitudes towards the concepts, it is important that the same people be maintained in these roles throughout the process, making them, in effect, team members. When, after a few weeks of concept refining, a new testing exercise is started, bringing in other researchers would naturally mean a serious waste of material and mental resources.

In a process in which focus is placed on testing rough ideas, there is no interest in testing final, and finely detailed, packaging. This aspect can be tested later, if then. The truth is that if the concept is appealing, packaging actually becomes secondary. It is one among many means of communication, rather than an end in itself. That is, of course, if there is any packaging at all! BSO created a huge following with nothing more than its logo, philosophy and people.

Experience shows that final research reports are nice for the archives and future reference, but they are never eagerly anticipated by those who see this sort of research as part of an ongoing creative process. Immediately the group sessions are over, the concepting team should be bursting with new ideas and feedback, which have to be quickly processed into new or modified proposals. They have no time for reports.

So, when does the consumer definitively embrace the concept? Well, in fact, it never happens during the research phase itself: good research results are never a guarantee of success. What the research shows is whether or not the concept 'clicks' and, of course, whether it meets with resistance. However, ultimate success itself can, unfortunately, only be ascertained by the brand's concept market performance.

It should also be stressed, however, that the fact that a group of consumers rejects a concept is no reason not to introduce it. Nowadays, opposing trends and tastes exist side by side, and it is very unusual for one single brand to attain complete market dominance – Heineken will never again have more than 50% of the Dutch market and IBM will remain one competitor among many. Companies should therefore change their aspirations: they should aim at introducing brands that are very appealing to 10% of consumers, rather than one that 50% of consumers consider 'quite nice'. Frequently, if 10% of consumers have a strong antipathy to a brand, there are usually another 10% who are crazy about it. Should research reveal this sort of polarisation, my advice would be: Introduce it! Obviously the brand will attract a lot of attention! The chance that it will eventually catch on with the 80% of initially non-committed consumers is excellent.

When Swatch watches were introduced, many somewhat older consumers saw them as being too 'young' and toy-like – which only served to strengthen their appeal to their core group. Today, more and more of the older people are jumping aboard the Swatch bandwagon: even businessmen can be found with three or four watches, which they wear on different occasions and with different outfits. Similarly, I believe that, if polled, 80% of managers would have rejected the Apple Macintosh concept prior to its introduction.

Lateral testing

Since there is no single correct answer in the concepting process and concepts arise from chance discoveries, it can be very revealing to actually test concepts with people who do not fit the following that concepters vaguely have in mind; for example, testing a cleaning concept brand only on men, or a product for the youth market on 40-year-olds, or vice versa. This is especially true at the beginning of the process, when the consumer is presented with a series of rough ideas. This not only elicits surprising reactions, but also could throw up new ideas for entirely new concepts. This sort of 'lateral' testing is a good example of how the research itself can become more integrated into the creative process – and more fun too.

7.2 Concept boards instead of production test facilities

The traditional product-development process often involves building new production test facilities – either separate or within existing facilities – before the product is tested or launched in the marketplace. This procedure makes sense for products that fall into the categories of genuine product development or genuine product innovations. Today, this would be the case in the telecommunications and computer sectors, but also in areas such as frozen-food production, where the necessary hygienic conditions can only be met by setting up a new production test facility. The viability of the technical production for such products must of course be assured.

Cosmetic innovation and concept brand products are another story altogether, however. Indeed, I feel that companies throw their money away investing in production test facilities in these cases.

Let us begin with cosmetic innovations. Companies all too often pour small fortunes, not to speak of their precious time, into tinkering with packaging details, new fragrances or some new line extension or other. Once this is over, the cosmetic innovations are run through a test, the results of which tell the company something about the consumer's response to the product's details – e.g. 'Light-blue cap scored better than red cap'. Nothing is learnt about the product proposition itself, that is, the consumer's reason for buying. In fact, very little knowledge is gained about the consumer at all. It is little wonder that 75% of these 'new products' are soon withdrawn from the shelves.

Concept brands involve a reverse process, as we have seen. Companies producing these products are more interested in focusing on the consumer than on the product – in concept boards rather than production test facilities. The company first invests in *communications*, which then leads to the refinement of concepts. The brands spring out of these, before any factory facility even exists. In fact, the company may never actually have any factories at all: Davidoff does not have any cigar-production facilities of its own, and most contemporary fashion brands subcontract all of their production.

The concepting approach may seem slow and expensive. It takes about nine months, during which the money seems to be spent only on the concepting team's (high) fees, travel and other expenses, and research costs. And the result? Merely some rough concept drafts. This might appear very extravagant, but compared with the expense of building production test lines, it is negligible. The value of successful drafts, when converted into successful brands, is immense. Furthermore, the collectively accumulated knowledge about consumer groups is itself a valuable asset in view of future exercises and development of new brands.

In comparison, a production test line whose product fails the consumer test winds up on the scrap heap, and the company has to start again from scratch. By focusing from the start on details, the company ends up empty handed if the product fails. Indeed, even if it succeeds, and a decision is made to introduce the product, it is remarkable how many planned introductions have to be postponed. This is usually because there is too much tinkering going on around the production itself.

After a well-planned concepting process, the company has a number of interesting concepts worked out on simple concept boards and is ready to go. If the general concepting basis is sound, the ultimate range of products can be enormous. Concepting's lateral thinking, communication, creativity and understanding of consumer behaviour provide the raw materials from which the brands and products are built.

It is also true that the products ultimately brought out under the concept brands frequently tend to be generic, fully developed or commoditised. A Calvin Klein T-shirt, for instance, is not exactly an innovative product. Similarly, BSO's consultants could be working with IBM, but when providing services under the BSO brand they give the client something different.

Further, as we have mentioned, concepting companies tend increasingly to subcontract production to third parties. If they do maintain production within the organisation, the best procedure for the company is to provide the production facility with independent management and make it into a separate profit centre; that is, regard it as much as possible as an external supplier. Heineken production facilities, for example, should ideally be 'supplying' product to the company's centre responsible for concept development (New Concept Development section), where the new brands would be developed. If these factories are unable to do so due to lack of capacity or any other reasons, there should be the possibility of shifting production to third parties without much delay. The producer that can most efficiently deliver the best quality deserves to be the one to work for the brand. If a producer proves to be a disappointment, it can be quickly replaced by another.

Naturally, since production facilities need time to prepare for production, the concepting company needs to establish contact with the possible production companies – be they internal or external – as soon as the new concepts start taking clear form. Using concept boards, they can explain and illustrate the brand and its concept to the possible producers. The latter can then get a good grasp, for example, of the reasons behind the need for specific quality requirements and why particular technical problems have to be solved – e.g. producing a weirdly shaped, purple bottle. This process allows the concepting company to test production feasibility, on the basis of the potential producer's culture as well as its technical capability, production quality, speed and capacity.

7.3 Early involvement of retailers

Some concept brands remain under the complete control of the brand owner from the moment they are introduced. This might involve the establishment of company-owned distribution networks such as The Body Shop has done, or a direct-writing system as in the case of Club Med and Eurocamp. Other brands, particularly the 'fast-moving' ones, require existing distribution channels by virtue of the nature of the products, which require wide, mass distribution.

Convincing retailers to take on new concept brands proceeds differently than with traditional product brands. Purchasing managers in these distribution channels are approached daily by manufacturers, pushing to get their various cosmetically innovated products onto the shelves. This persuasion process usually takes place at the end of the product-development process: the product is ready, the packaging design is done and it is all backed up by the requisite research proving, for example, that '68% of housewives would definitely buy the product if it were on the store shelves'. It is not surprising that retailers react somewhat sceptically to these claims, since they are more than aware that 75% of these cosmetic innovations ultimately flop. Nor is it surprising that they are now considering demanding 'flop reimbursement' from producers for these types of products.

How different purchasers' attitudes are when, under a concepting approach, they are consulted and involved in developing rough ideas for brands earlier in the game! They can thus contribute their very valuable experience and knowledge of the consumer as input to the new brand concept. No longer simply targets of sales pitches, they become *partners*, contributing all their resources in the process of constructing the concept, and even, if interested, participating in the later development stages. Just as it draws in consumers, concepting thus also incorporates retailers – precisely because of their understanding of consumers. The central theme is openness and participation rather than late-in-the-day 'product pushing'.

Further, companies that genuinely involve their potential retailing partners in the concepting process also benefit from some extremely important inside information. For example, they can evaluate the willingness of these partners to eventually take on a product early on in the game, even in the absence of hard-and-fast agreements. More importantly, the production process starts up only after agreements have been reached regarding the initial production quantities. This is in contrast to the normal sequence of producing the desired volume, building up stocks and then 'pushing' the goods.

The inclusion of retailers should also bring with it a new approach to sales and margin forecasting. Currently, the usual marketing practice is to set sales projections far in advance. They tend to be extremely ambitious, particularly with regard to their time-frame: huge sales figures are expected very quickly, with corresponding gains in market share and profitability. Experience shows this approach to be quite unrealistic. The targets tend to be far too ambitious, the forecasts too rosy; worst of all, the consumer does not always perceive the innovations to be such. Within a short period of time, disappointment sets in. By following this approach, companies set themselves up for disappointment.

In any event, concepting cannot use such an approach. The attitude or vision that is the concept is built up using small core groups of consumers, before being spread to a broader following. This implies that retailers will be expected to *start small and expand slowly*. If the retailer is a believer in the concept – and thus ready to be a partner in it – then it should be willing to accept slow growth with a view to success in the medium or even long term. Naturally this might be an expensive proposition, but it is better to go slow and attain solid growth. Further, since production is usually outsourced, there is no need for the company to produce huge volumes at the outset: the third party produces increased volumes as required.

The best retail company purchasers rarely object to the concepting approach. Accustomed to dealing with producers' sales pitches and push for shelf space for their latest cosmetic innovations – and with the disappointing results of three out of four of these in terms of pre-established sales targets – they often find the concepting approach refreshing. After all, here are producers who do not demand that much shelf space, and do not impose their ideas about which competing product should make room for theirs. Concept brands thus are often welcomed. All they need is a relatively modest shelf allotment, though for a longer period, with the *possibility* of future expansion. Given the development background of concept brands (particularly if the retailer has been involved), the case for their ultimate success is stronger, and good retailers realise this: they have a keen sense of which products will probably flop and which succeed.

The 1990s have witnessed a number of discussions and arguments about the shift of power along the product chain, from (cosmetic-innovation) producers to retailers. In a concepting context this issue is irrelevant, since the brand itself has the power. It is beyond the pushing and shoving in the frenetic struggle for oversaturated markets. Indeed, good concept brands will ultimately have enough 'pull' to ensure that the demand of their increasing following will continue to grow on its own. How much push, for example, would Diesel need if it were given even a modest amount of space in a department store? The brand itself has the power, it will do the work: the producer or retailer can stand aside.

It is true that by starting small, the concepting approach runs the serious risk of stock-outs and missed sales opportunities. However, this should not concern good concepting companies and their retailers too much. They realise that 'sold out' spells 'popular'. It is a strong signal that the concept is 'clicking' and production should be stepped up: it indicates that there is a durable profit potential just around the corner. While 'sold out' for 'me too' brands means that consumers will probably turn to the competition, for a concept brand this is much less likely. A concept brand's consumers, its following, would rather wait a couple of days to get what they really want.

Chapter 8
Communicating a Concept

Under concepting, brands seek to convey concepts of various sorts and dimensions, such as visions, ideas, attitudes and convictions. As we have seen, this implies an approach to the market that is governed by communications. Though important, the other elements – or the other Ps: product, price and place – remain secondary, and indeed are managed in part as communication platforms for the brand.

This chapter examines the following elements that are key in successfully communicating a concept:

- *The concept statement*
- *Internal communications*
- *Total communications*
- *'Unplanned' communications*
- *Patient communications*
- *Natural growth*
- *Continuous communications and feedback*
- *Non-complacent communications*

8.1 Concept statement: concept and behaviour code

Before the brand can be defined, its concept must be established. In other words, the first step is to identify a vision, a 'wavelength', a 'world', etc. for the brand. Whether it is born in the mind of a particular person or as a result of a concepting team's work, the first internal product in the concepting process is the statement describing the concept.

This concept statement expresses what the concept brand 'feels' and 'thinks', what it stands for, and its inherent norms and values. In other words, it is the brand's editorial formula or its statement of principles. The statement is accompanied by the brand's behaviour code. Statement and code together guide all of the brand's communications.

The concept statement therefore refers to mental or abstract elements – the brand's 'roots', for example – not to product characteristics. The reasons a particular brand name is chosen to embody the concept should be apparent. Good examples of this are Toys R Us, Häagen Dazs and Planet Hollywood.

The concept statement also contains a draft of the brand's *behaviour code*, which answers questions such as: How will the brand behave in different kinds of situations? What types of events or causes will it support? Will it engage in price wars? How politically correct will it be? How formal or casual will it be? How will it portray the company's employees, if at all? What sort of distribution channels will it use?

The details of the code are crucial because the brand's concept is contained and communicated in *every* aspect of its behaviour in society. In other words, *all of the brand's behaviour is communication* – not just its advertising. The code ensures the behavioural consistency necessary for strong concept brands.

In most instances, concept brands emerge from a single, simple vision. Steve Job's concept of a small, handy, user-friendly personal computer is a case in point. Upon the introduction of the Macintosh in 1984, Apple's concept statement was presumably further refined with regard to the brand's style of communication and behaviour on the market. Apple's motto became: 'For the rest of us'.

The concept statement of Richard Branson's Virgin would also be simple: 'Rebelliousness is healthy for business: giving the establishment a hard time is not only fun, it's important. And playfulness and dreaming is not incompatible with adulthood.'

The resulting defiant-underdog aura has created a wide and growing following for Virgin; a following that embraces various consumers in many lines of businesses.

BSO also kept it simple. The company believed that, as computer consultants, they could never really be 'shoulder-to-shoulder' with clients if their personnel were all located in one spot, from where they were sent out 'on missions' to clients. The physical distance also created a psychological distance from the client. Moreover, by clustering the consultants at headquarters, there was a tendency for them to spend far too much time on office matters – dealing with procedures, attending meetings and pushing paper. Founder Eckard Wintzen's vision was of a tight consultant–client relationship, of 'user-friendly' consultants, who would ideally even come from the same neighbourhood as their clients. To this end, BSO followed a so-called cell system, whereby its offices were allowed to grow to 50 employees, at which point a new office – a (cloned) cell of the first – would be set up. In this way a network of 50 to 60 offices developed, first in the Netherlands, and then elsewhere in Europe and abroad. BSO's concept statement referred to a particular management philosophy, and actually had nothing to do with computerisation as such.

The recently launched Smart car also embodies a simple concept: 'Reduce to the max!' Smart offers solutions for mobility. The tiny Smart car is a great solution for people living in urban agglomerations in which driving and finding a parking place is an annoying part of their daily routine. Furthermore, when the Smart driver has to fly to other European cities, a Smart car will be arranged for – at reduced rates, of course. Smart delivers solutions to all forms of mobility: when needed, Smart drivers can change their car for a bigger one. 'Reduce to the max!' is not only focused on the car itself. Smart produces its vehicles in its northern French plant with as little environmental impact as possible. Smart has also recently introduced Smart clothes and other merchandise – the Smart concept field is wide. Perhaps they will also get into reducing home appliances to the max!

There is an interesting comparison to be made between a concept statement and a mission statement one finds printed in annual reports. In the case of the Smart car, for example, a mission statement might read: 'Smart wants to acquire x% of the small-car market'. Does this have a distinctive, motivational impact on employees and consumers? Does it really tell us anything about which direction the company wants to go in? Compare it with what might be its concept statement: 'If we want to go on living as we have up till now, we will have to adjust. We will offer an individual mobility concept. Smart is the symbol of the common European future.'

8.2 Internal communications: constant and multi-directional

The first communication objective is to make sure the concepting company itself fully understands and 'feels' the essence of the concept. Internal communications are key in this regard.

When a new concepting company is set up, the attitudes, convictions and ambitions of potential employees should be carefully considered. Selection should be based on their willingness – indeed keenness – to participate in the process of developing, supporting and implementing the concept. Particularly during the first phase, everyone needs to be motivated to spread the brand and the underlying concept. This does not mean that the staff should be made up of 'yes men'. Although the *brand's* behaviour code is established, how staff members, in a good enterprising atmosphere, should behave to promote the concept should generally be left up to them. This means allowing them a reasonable amount of latitude. Too much hammering-on about 'do's and don't's' invariably backfires. Of course, subservient individuals will adapt, but the most creative spirits will feel that they are being held back, and will probably start looking for greener pastures.

All of the above also applies to cases where a new concept brand is being developed within an existing company. As we have seen, the concepting team should be perceived as a start-up company and be given all the autonomy and space it needs. If the team is forced to follow existing company procedures and abide by its culture, at worst, the whole effort will fail, and, at best, it will be plagued by frustration and delays.

There are various forms of internal communications that ensure staff become true partners in radiating the concept. Getting up on a soapbox and addressing staff is one of them; indeed, good leadership is characterised by its frequent use of this option. However, such one-way communications is usually not enough in a company wishing to maintain a healthy entrepreneurial spirit. Preventing the development of a fragmented-group culture and ensuring there is plenty of communication between staff in an informal climate is just as important. Very helpful in this regard are the staff 'road trips' to mix with consumers and even to visit other concepting companies – Diesel does this, for example. Ultimately, with the growth of the concept, other means such as magazines, intranet and the internet also become important.

Handbooks that set down the details of a brand's communications – such as those favoured in international marketing organisations – are definitely to be avoided. Their purpose is to harness staff and restrict their liberty with the incomprehensible goal of creating uniformity across national boundaries. The result is brand petrifaction, as companies focus more on internal communications means than the end. Good concepting companies, like Diesel or The Body Shop, would be very unlikely to fall into this trap: all that matters to them is their concept statement.

8.3 Total communications: encompassing all behaviour

We have seen that in a concepting company the main focus is on communications, and brand behaviour in all its variations constitutes communications. When compared with previous

approaches, the main changes represented by 'total communications' are:

- From 'integrated communications' to consistent behaviour
- From 'theme' to 'statement'
- From seduction to mentality sharing

To begin with, communications is no longer considered a
separate, isolated activity that is undertaken once the product-
development phase is completed. In the past, under this product-
focused approach, the purpose of communications – that is, the
advertising campaign – was to add values. Other means of
communications and tools were developed separately – often by
different people in separate outside agencies – with various
specific goals in mind, e.g. boosting Christmas sales of a whisky
brand or improving a company's image in the capital market.
During the 1980s, many companies realised that this approach
was leading to a splitting of their brand's personality. Their
response was 'integrated communications': all elements had to be
brought together again in a unified, common image.

From a concepting perspective, integration is never an issue,
because the communication elements never become segmented in
the first place. The concept brand's position is established *once
and definitively* at its very conception; thereafter, communications
based on the brand's behaviour code is pursued, with consistency
as the guiding principle.

In its battle against brand split personality, integrated communications strives for as much unity of communication form and
content as possible. The *campaign theme* becomes all-determining
in establishing the brand image in all communications, from
advertising, to folders, to store materials. This can work very well
for companies that aim to achieve the aura of a high-quality,
reliable and efficient organisation. KLM, for example, has
established such an aura with its 'blue sky territory' in this way.
Coca-Cola has actually done the same by claiming its red colour.

Total communications, on the other hand, focuses on conveying
the concept to the market, and uses all types of brand behaviour
to this end. While in classical brand philosophy the brand's

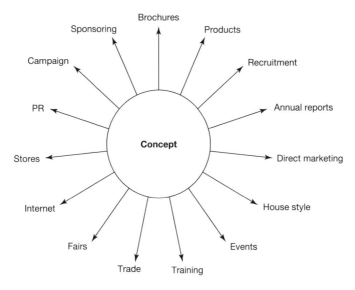

Figure 8.1 The wide embrace of total communications.

theme, its main message, is largely relegated to the media campaign, in total communications every piece of communication embodies the concept statement. In other words, the message of the concept statement radiates consistently in every aspect of the brand's behaviour. Figure 8.1 represents the case of the total communications of the various behavioural elements of a brand and their connection with the central concept.

The ultimate objective of total communications, of course, is to create as large a following as possible for the concept. This renders obsolete a number of traditional ideas, such as building the brand 'above the line', selling it 'below the line' and 'pull and push' – relics of an age when advertising was merely a means of seducing the public. Under concepting, the point is rather to have the public share in the brand's mentality: because they are part of the brand, there is no seduction necessary.

Consequently, the repeated communication of the concept is not limited to the form of the superficial features of a campaign image. In fact any form is permissible, as long as the message being communicated fits the concept exactly and is consistent.

Aad Muntz, head of Dutch insurer Centraal Beheer, put it this way: 'The key to good communication is not repetition but consistency.'

Actually, the notion of brand behaviour also makes the term 'brand personality' eminently sensible. The analogy is also useful because brands should have – like humans – personalities that are variable and multifaceted, though the person remains the same: how boring and uninteresting people and brands would be if they had only one way of speaking, acting and reacting. I believe that this sentiment is becoming increasingly widespread in Western industrialised countries. Specifically, I am convinced that consumers are increasingly demanding brands that are interesting; that have personality.

This conviction was clearly confirmed to me in recent extensive discussions that I had with young adults (aged between 20 and 30 years) in 18 large cities of ten European countries. Their message was clear: they categorically reject thematic campaigns which constantly project the same image. Thus campaigns that carefully follow the precepts of integrated communications are scoffed at by this group as too boring and cautious – read meaningless and unchallenging. They are dismissed as 'standing for nothing' and being 'the usual corporate crap'.

What young people want is to be stimulated, entertained and amused by a brand. They want to be able to get in touch with it – though this rarely happens, the point is that *that* is their desire. They want brands that stand for and mean something; that surprise, entertain, challenge and respect them.

What is more, I do not believe that this change in the expectations regarding communications is uniquely confined to the young. This rejection (or apathy) affects – or will soon affect – the whole of society: it is a natural response to an overdose of slick, visual saturation campaigns. Even when the campaigns grab people's attention, they never inspire them – they are often compared with wallpaper: just stuck there; part of the furniture.

The group discussions confirmed a parallel conviction about Western industrial societies: material goods are in overabundance and there is a real and growing need for substance. Brands can satisfy this by providing conviction and truly standing for something. Consumers also seem keen on making a fresh start, of being part of a new beginning. Concepting participates in this process. In a sense, its purpose is to produce meaningful brands to fill the gaps in people's lives; gaps that have emerged partly as a result of the decline of traditional religious, political and family values. Traditional brand approaches cannot fill this identity vacuum.

8.4 'Unplanned' communications: going with the flow

Total communications does not necessarily imply intensive communication. Timeliness and targeting are its hallmarks: communicating at the right time and in the right place to convey the concept.

This implies an entirely new perspective on the process of communication planning. The traditional process is based on specific, quantified goals – e.g. 80% name recognition, 40% of the target group sees brand as standing for 'expertise', 15% of them to receive trial samples during the campaign; the underlying notion being that the goals are attainable by a particular point in time, and the market and consumer can be manipulated to this end. The effort is then launched, usually using the mass media for the most part. Typically, however, this is followed a few months later by a post-mortem to try to understand why the (often unrealistic) goals were not reached.

Concepting planning is more open-ended; it evolves along with the concept, going with the brand's flow. Ben Cohen and Jerry Greenfield subtitled the book on their ice-cream company *How to Run a Values-Led Business and Make Money Too*.[1] This nicely captures the premise of communication planning under concepting: the first priority is the conveyance of a concept – in this case, particular values – and commercial objectives are secondary. The fact is, however, if the first component is well-implemented, the second will follow almost automatically. What this means is that concepting-companies take a (difficult) 'open-minded'

---

1. B. Cohen and J. Greenfield (1998) *Ben & Jerry's Double-Dip: How to Run a Values-Led Business and Make Money Too*. New York: Simon & Schuster.

approach to their communication planning, which might even be termed 'unplanned'. The future development of their commercial position is left vague: it will grow along with the expansion of the brand's following.

This open-mindedness also applies to the details of the communication planning. This, for example, means that 'top-down' media planning is replaced by an approach amounting to being present in the market in all kinds of ways and at different times, depending on circumstances. Probably only a small portion of the 'communication budget' – a term that suddenly has a very outdated ring to it – will actually be allocated in advance. Most of it, in fact, will remain 'open', to be used at the most opportune moment: e.g. coat-tailing on particular events, responding to breaking news, participating in a special annual report, or sponsoring occasions and phenomena that are consistent with the brand's concept and appeal to its following. Behaviour once regarded disdainfully as opportunistic becomes a central creative component under concepting communications.

Since, under concepting, the brand begins small, as a kernel, there is no need initially to employ the heavy communication artillery. Investments in communications can grow in step with the brand's market performance. In fact, the current concept brands seem to have a view of media campaigns as being the icing on the communication cake, rather than the cake itself. Most communication resources are funnelled into other activities.

Let us look at some concrete examples of the concepting approach to communication planning.

- Although its famous 'For successful living' campaign has only been around since about 1991, Diesel is very selective about its advertising. This selective media planning 'only' serves to strengthen its philosophy which has been maintained and carried out in many other ways for years.

- Corona beer, during the early years following its introduction in Europe, hardly advertised at all. All the Mexican company did was make sure that the product was available at all public partying spots that were likely to attract the brand's potential following, and where the curious, quasi-mystical ritual surrounding the lime in the bottle could grow into a code for those 'in the know'. One cannot be certain about such things of course, but I wonder whether Corona would have been as successful if it had taken the usual mass-media campaign approach.

- When British Airways hit upon the ingenious idea to have various artists repaint the tails of all its aircraft, Virgin's Richard Branson quickly had his fleet decorated with the very British flag his competitor had chosen to scrap. The action must have involved digging deeply into the company's communications pocket, but it attracted just as much, if not more, front-page attention as BA's move a few weeks earlier. Once again, Virgin had reinforced its rebellious attitude.

- In the early 1990s, BSO began investing heavily in its annual report. This included introducing an estimate of the environmental damage caused by the company's activities and a discussion as to how it should compensate society in this regard. This last element was reason enough for widespread coverage of the report on editorial pages. BSO's unique ecological consciousness was also communicated in the report's award-winning design. This led to further exposure for the brand – not to speak of strengthened staff motivation. Naturally, the report was planned, but the media exposure was not. Such a phenomenon cannot be quantified or predicted. In this case it was a very valuable consequence of the company's reflecting its concept in all aspects of the brand's behaviour.

- Apple's famous '1984' one-time commercial during the Super Bowl transmission is a classic example of concepting's opportunistic communication approach. In this case, the big communication artillery was certainly rolled out: the spot cost $6 million, for one, highly effective blast. The commercial shows a young female athlete running into a huge hall carrying a large sledge-hammer. She races past rows of grim, apathetic workers staring at a huge screen in front of them, as if hypnotised. The clear message was that 'big brother' had transformed them into the faceless drones strikingly described in George Orwell's *1984*. The woman launches the sledge-hammer at the screen, which shatters into a million pieces. A calming voice-over assures us: '1984 won't be like *1984*'. The sensational attack on IBM was unmistakable. For months thereafter the newspapers could not write enough about it. Those who had not seen it found themselves desperately trying to get a copy of the commercial. They need not have worried, though: both the commercial and Macintosh got comprehensive, free airing thanks to the television talk shows.

The skill of spotting opportunities of this sort and assessing the impact of such well-timed action is key to concepting communications. Being present at the right time and at the right place is essential. As the Apple case shows, this does not necessarily imply small-scale actions. The proper dosage varies from situation to situation. It all depends on the brand, the type of concept, the potential following and, of course, the resources available.

Obviously, good decisions regarding when and where to act require a completely dedicated concepting team that knows that ivory-tower thinking is a prescription for paralysis. As good concepters, they have to relish uncertainty and are constantly alert to and aware of trends and events affecting the following.

8.5 Patient communications: waiting for the oil to spread

During talks over the past few years with marketing and communication professionals, I would start to describe concepting to them and was occasionally interrupted by someone who would say: 'Oh, you mean niche marketing?'

No, concepting is not niche marketing. Niche marketing is very clearly about defining a target group within a larger market segment, and then trying to appeal to it. The market for designer furniture – e.g. a two-person sofa priced at £6000 – is a niche-market within the overall furniture market. It is as easy to picture the type of buyer as it is to picture the glossy magazines that showcase such goods. Nor, of course, is concepting mainstream marketing. The point about concepting is that it may *result* in a following that has niche or mass dimensions, but such a result is never part of the original objective. The ultimate nature of the following is determined by the concept itself: as its 'oil' slowly spreads, the nature and dimensions of its market become apparent.

Thus, even though concepting does not work with pre-delineated target groups, it might very well lead to a niche or a mainstream brand. The size of the concept brand's following will ultimately be determined by the concept itself and the assortment of articles that can be sold in its field.

This unpredictability of a concept's fate is particularly well exemplified by the Montignac example; a concept that is today growing prodigiously. However, who could have predicted this? The diet-method's success has led to the sale of Montignac cookbooks, books on its healthy-living concept, a growing number of food products, as well as special cooking utensils, and memberships to local Montignac clubs and tickets for public readings. A glance at the www.montignac.com site strikingly demonstrates how rapidly the Montignac method has grown from its humble Dutch beginnings in 1996 to a worldwide phenomenon threatening the established position of an organisation like Weight Watchers.

Montignac also demonstrates that in our communication-oriented age the oil can spread very quickly; that patient communication does not necessarily mean having to wait a long time for results. Though a rapid spread is usually good news, of course, it can also create bottlenecks and management problems. This was Ikea's experience during its first year in the Netherlands. The store attracted such a tidal wave of customers that its parking facilities could not cope, goods were sold-out for months at a time, and people actually fainted while waiting in the long checkout queues. This of course resulted in enormous publicity, which led to even larger waves of customers.

Thus, although concepting means starting small on the basis of a core group, it certainly does not entail staying small or staying small for long. Ultimately, whether or not a brand becomes 'mainstream' – that is, a big brand with a large following, such as Marlboro, McDonald's or Ikea – depends on the size of the current or attainable 'consumption pattern', and the attractiveness of the concept.

Once the following becomes more defined, it is of course up to the company to exploit the product possibilities the concept field offers. This depends on the ambitions of the company. Some concept brands offer wide product fields, but the companies owning them do not exploit them to the extent they could. In other words, the following is open to consume concept brand products, but these are simply not supplied. Thus although margins for concept brands – whether catering to niches or to the mainstream – tend to be very attractive, some companies could improve their performance through a better understanding of their following.

8.6   Natural growth: patience and readiness

Communications under concepting is premised on the natural spread of the concept and growth of a following. Experience has shown that a good concepting process takes about nine months to produce the first concepts. Nine months: from conception to baby. However, as in humans, this is only the first part of a long journey.

At birth, the baby is still very vulnerable. It can hardly walk and cannot speak. The concepters, the parents of this newborn wonder, must be conscious of the fact that the hard work of raising the child lies ahead. Concept brands call for a completely different perspective of time than most companies have been used to when introducing new products to the market.

The traditional perspective is hectic and rushed. As we have seen, target setting becomes an obsession. The product must attain a certain measure of financial success within a predetermined period of time. We often speak of periods ranging from a year to a few years, but, in fact, especially in consumer goods marketing, anything over a year is rare. In fact, companies typically expect a new product to earn back its introduction costs as quickly as possible and sometimes even to show a profit in its first year. Budgets are allocated on the basis of various performance projections. These expectations play a major role with regard to: what percentage of the target group is to be penetrated, the size of the target group, repeat-purchase frequency, distribution, etc. They also form the basis for the company's plans for optimising the product's distribution, shelf-space, sales organisation and communication plan. Then the introduction begins. Should the results along the way somehow turn out to be disappointing, any and all kinds of actions are taken in an attempt to reach the goal, whatever the cost. The push begins: costs rise, and profits are further postponed.

By following this kind of game plan, companies effectively set up their new products or brands to fail – the bar is unrealistically high. Why, one may ask, is this short-term approach favoured so often? The most frequent answer points to the retailers. Power has shifted down the product chain from producers to retailers; and retailers want to see fast turnover and returns. A supermarket chain, for example, can decide the fate of the products on its shelves: a shaky beginning might mean the product is cut.

However, is it really fair to blame the supermarkets and other retailers? After all, was it not the producer who made the glorious sales pitch on the basis of spectacular projections – which it evidently believed in – in the first place? Is the new product really so extraordinary that the sales projections can realistically be met? Are those few TV spots, aimed at reaching housewives an average of 2.5 times, and the half-page ad in the supermarket magazine really enough to actually persuade the housewife to pick up the 'new' product? Is it not the producer who always insists on maximum shelf-space? When this space allocation turns out to be far too large to be profitable, whose fault is it?

'Oh come on now', might be the riposte, 'Shelf-space is essential to guarantee product visibility and ensure sales power.' My response would be: 'Isn't *that* the crux of the matter? Obviously you're counting on the *shelf's* pull: it is apparently stronger than that of the brand itself? Doesn't that speak volumes about the weakness of the proposition? A shelf does not make a brand. The brand is made in the mind of the consumer, and this takes *time*.' Ultimately, the brand can acquire such power that it completely contradicts the notion of the producer–retailer power-shift – for example, supermarkets will probably bend over backwards to *offer* Montignac or Ben & Jerry's prime shelf-space.

Why is it that we raise and nurture children for at least 16 years after their birth, while we allow our fragile new brands to sink or swim, or leave them entirely in the hands of their foster parents, known as retailers? Are we not just choosing the easy way out by dumping them at the side of the road with a few sandwiches to see them through a few days, in the hope that they will be able to find their own way, or that some passerby will take them along?

When, as in concepting, one begins with communications as the starting point, one has to get it absolutely right. After all, if the concept does not catch on, all is lost. If, because of resource constraints, the communications cannot be conducted on a national scale, the concepter simply has to make a smart choice, choosing the optimal approach. This might mean beginning with a region or a city, or, for instance, with a single (highly collaborative) retail channel. A beginning can even be made without a retailer, as in the case of Eurocamp, or with an own retail channel (Ikea) or franchise network (Benetton). Actually, fashion brands often insist on doing their own distribution, so as to determine the aura around its brand: the concepter is not at the mercy of the whim, lack of understanding, impatience or divergent interests of third parties. Lastly, the internet also offers a *virtual* starting point for the introduction of new concept brands and a means of reaching users worldwide.

If the concept meets with success with its core group, then the oil can begin to spread. However, the concepter must be nimble-footed, and be ready to change course quickly. A healthy dose of self-criticism is also necessary to make clear assessments of whether the task has been successfully completed in one area before moving on to the next. If care is not taken, there is a chance that both the old and the new areas will not be given the full, 100% attention they need and deserve. This can produce sudden trouble.

Careful account should also be taken of the human resources required. These needs will grow along with the concept's successful spread, and the company has to be prepared to respond, particularly with regard to its human resources. The concepting team must be able to expand apace. The new people must truly identify with the concept before they are sent to represent it in the new area of expansion. In sum, patience and readiness are the key words for controlled and sustained growth.

Success under concepting is therefore not measured on the basis of a particular point in time following introduction, but at consecutive intervals. If things go very well, there is even a chance that the success will 'overstretch' the brand. This is not surprising in a communication age in which people are extremely mobile and the media's reach far outstrips the brand's starting space. To refer again to our earlier examples, the opening of the first Ikea store in the Netherlands and the resultant traffic jams made the national news more than once, thus automatically boosting the brand's following. Montignac's diet also became a national story, leading to an increased following and frantic efforts to reprint the books and boost supply of special-food products. BSO, too, grew so fast that the company had problems finding the right people to provide good service to its growing client base and ensure its new office clones were well-managed.

In any event, initial patience is rewarded. When controlled growth is planned from the beginning, at a certain point things are very likely to cruise along automatically. The child has then obviously grown out of puberty and is increasingly able to find its own way in the world. Because the concept welcomes an ever-larger number of followers, their impact as concept ambassadors becomes more and more important. Sometimes the message is passed on by word of mouth. This was clearly the case with Montignac, a brand that is hardly ever advertised. Many Apple followers are also passionate brand ambassadors, if not soldiers, in the battle against Microsoft. At other times the brand is passed or taken over through unspoken communication and observation:

one person sees another buying the brand and gets the urge to take part in the brand as well. This phenomenon is especially frequent with young people, among whom brand success can quickly snowball. Nike and Diesel, but also cigarette and drink brands, have benefited from these non-verbal brand transfers: many people smoke Marlboro Lights or drink Corona simply because others do.

Although growth rates will vary from case to case, it is clear that one year is not long enough for a concept brand to mature. Brands such as Benetton, Ikea, Red Bull and Swatch have all existed for more than ten years. If H&M fashions still seem young in the Netherlands, remember that it took years of brand development in Scandinavia before it expanded into the 'new' Dutch region. Perhaps the exceptional cases of Montignac and Dr Atkins earlier diet revolution moved along so much faster because dieting is probably second only to the weather as a favourite topic of conversation.

8.7 Continuous communications: flourishing on feedback

We have seen how a successful concepting company introduces a concept and allows it to be spread by an increasingly large following, whose identification with the brand grows stronger over time. In essence, concepting involves the establishment of the following equation: *consumer = concept = company*.

This implies that communications among the three elements is central to concepting. By this I mean communications involving the company's staff, suppliers and the brand following. All need to be continuously and positively reinforced and their input listened to; after all, they all constitute important players in the process of extending the following. It is fundamental also that the communications be multi-directional. Particularly those consumers identifying with the brand see themselves as part of a large family, and want to communicate and give feedback to the brand's originators. They want to express their own views, to ask questions and to criticise, constructively or not.

A good concepting company will value consumer contacts highly and it will go to great lengths to encourage them. Constant contact with consumers – be they followers, hesitators or opponents – always produces new insights into the concept, which can help explain its performance and, if necessary, strengthen it. It also provides information about how consumer perceptions and patterns of living are changing, how the following relates to the brand philosophy and its products, as well as more detailed information, like distribution-channel preferences.

In other words, the more communication and feedback, the more the concepting team can ensure that the brand attains the maximum following and maintains its position by remaining on the consumers' 'wavelength'. This is a daily exercise; in fact, it is a sort of ongoing research, keeping everyone sharp and on his or her toes, while also providing inspiration for future moves.

The Dutch teenage magazine *Break Out!* embodies this principle perfectly. It is the first of its kind: it is actually put together with the help of its readers. Instead of cover girls gracing its pages, the readers themselves are pictured. The editorial staff do not determine which pop-world news will be featured on the cover, the readers do: if they want to see the Backstreet Boys on the cover ten weeks in a row, then that is exactly what they will get. The editors have opted for the role of intermediaries, or a passive creative platform, for their readers' wishes. Every week they send out 2000 questionnaires along with the magazine and every week readers send over 1000 back. The readers thus take *Break Out!* seriously, because the magazine takes them seriously. By Dutch publishing standards, the concept is a great success: after its first year it has already reached a circulation of 80,000.

The impact of feedback communications is not surprising to most concepting companies. An afternoon's surfing on the internet reveals that almost all concept brands have outstanding interactive sites; they are exciting, entertaining, up to date and active. Invitations to 'please join' or 'please react' appear frequently. Nike, Diesel, Benetton, Ben & Jerry's, Club Med and Smart all have top-quality interactive sites. Their sites offer the potential follower exactly what he or she wants: the brand's beliefs and convictions, background philosophies, complete biographical descriptions with pictures of the founders (including information about their private lives), as well as examples of campaign visuals and all sorts of additional information and *lots* of fun. By means of 'virtual clubs' the brand's followers can even communicate with each other. Web surfers who venture into these sites cannot help but get the feeling that everything is out in the open, that they can take a peek behind the scenes. They are made to feel valued, fully fledged individuals who are on the same level as the company behind the brand. They can genuinely feel they are 'members of the club': 'The company, the brand: they are you!'

Interactivity can be promoted in a host of other ways of course: from magazines, such as *Greenpeace,* and other feedback mechanisms long used by clubs and other associations. It can also be embodied in particular individuals, usually the brand creators, who often devote a great deal of their personal attention to their following and to the media. For example, they attend special events and give talks, where they interact with the media and the followers, and where they are able to pick up a lot more information than many a research study could come up with. This happened, for example, when Virgin Vodka was recently launched in the Netherlands, and the highly publicised presence of the brand's creator, Richard Branson, became the centre of the campaign.

8.8 Non-complacent communications: no wallowing in success

Many will be familiar with the company success stories in Tom Peters and Robert Waterman, Jr's best-selling *In Search of Excellence: Lessons From America's Best-Run Companies.*[2] A few years after the book came out, half of these 'blue chip' companies, such as IBM, were in big trouble. One of the basic reasons for their problems is also well-known: it is tough making an effort

---

2.   T. Peters and R. Waterman, Jr (1982) *In Search of Excellence: Lessons from America's Best-Run Companies.* New York: Harper & Row.

when one is at the top. Once successful, companies have – perhaps a very human – tendency to coast, to take things easier for a while and enjoy the success. One tell-tale sign of this is when people start talking of the need for changes in communications. Statements like: 'We are entering a brand new phase now', can be an indirect request by employees to take things a bit easier, or it may indicate a suppressed desire or need for institutionalised structures and behaviour patterns.

Companies that become complacent become vulnerable. They begin to underestimate the competition and ignore or scoff at newcomers. Then, one fine day, they wake up and realise their mistake – but it is often too late.

Heineken, enjoying a privileged market position, was too late in realising the attractiveness to consumers of the more exclusive imported beers. IBM considered the IBM clones inferior to the originals and of little substance. Philips, once the primary supplier of consumer telephonic equipment, today hardly plays any part in the rapidly changing (commodity) market for portable and trendy phones.

While underestimating the competition, many of these companies also become a little too relaxed with their purse-strings; they acquire new plush buildings, additional departments and layers of management. They thereby lose their litheness, their market orientation, and slowly but surely are metamorphosed into large sloths.

The moral is that success should never be seen as the goal, but as a sign that the company is on the right track. This applies of course to every type of business, but is specially relevant for concepting companies. As we have seen, these firms are particularly dependent on continuous and direct contact with their followers. A company is successful not because it reaches a particular point or goal, but because it has good concepts and has created a continuous interactive communication process with its following. This very interaction, based on surprising and entertaining one another, keeps the brand and the following alive. Continuous communication is at the heart of a concept brand's success.

Once a brand starts growing, it is absolutely necessary to continue the one-to-one relationship that characterised the relationship with the core group at the very beginning. This is easiest for retailers, such as The Body Shop or McDonald's. The store facilitates regular contact with customers and it can also serve as a medium for a variety of brand-related messages, e.g. McDonald's place mats explaining the company's recycling process. Here are some other cases:

- Diesel provides a good model of continuous contact, this time by the concept founder himself, Renzo Rosso, who still makes his weekly flights around the world to exchange ideas with his following and to give the media his views on the world of fashion.
- Ikea's founder, Ingvar Kamprad, now in his 70s, who still shows up at the company every day, introduced an 'anti-bureaucracy' week in the company. During this week, managers are required to work in the Ikea stores themselves. He must have felt that things were beginning to go wrong, that managers were losing touch.
- To maintain contact with their followings, companies often use own magazines, which, naturally, are in close harmony with the brand's concept – e.g. Benetton's *Colors* and *Greenpeace*.

As mentioned earlier, the internet is becoming a more and more important medium for the following's communication with the brand. Good web-sites prove that the company is maintaining its alertness, sensitivity and involvement, even if the brand is getting on in years.

The larger a company gets, the more important communications within it becomes. It takes time and money to get new employees to truly grasp all the subtleties of the concept. Many of the means used to communicate outside the company are of course also effective. Benetton's *Colors*, for example, is also read by its franchisees all over the world; and BSO's recruitment advertisements also serve to constantly remind its employees of the company's philosophy.

The most important internal communication medium, however, is undoubtedly the brand's concept statement, which all new employees are made familiar with, and which they have to fully embrace as their own. The person's full and genuine conviction regarding the brand is indispensable if she or he is to fit in. Disney represents a typical case: employees who are not willing to perform in line with the company's concept are simply told to look for work elsewhere. The company's concept statement becomes the employees' bible, to be kept in the top draw of the desk or even next to the bed.

As already discussed, good internal communications also depends on company leaders being in frequent contact with staff. They should often get up on the soap-box to keep everyone updated on the concept's development, point out where mistakes were made, and generally keep the spotlight on the concept. Facts and figures can also be provided in this communication, but they should by no means constitute the main topic of discussion: they are no more than the result of spreading the word, and are far from being the only measures of success.

These occasions should also be used to give staff the chance to voice criticism and to make suggestions. Such feedback broadens the shared knowledge base and strengthens motivation. If things go according to plan, all those involved will feel as though they 'co-own' the brand, and will accompany the brand's life in the outside world and experience the public's reaction to it.

The growth of a concept brand ideally happens when all the people who have grown along with its core are able to develop into fully fledged concept ambassadors in the outside world. The more internal fellow concepters there are who can get the word out with the right tone, the greater the chance is that growth will also be qualitatively appropriate to the concept.

Good concepting companies do all they can to avoid vertical growth, i.e. setting up various departments and increasing the number of organisational layers. This process constitutes the first step towards inward-directedness, usually entailing a corresponding turning away from the outside world. Since one of the guiding principles of a concepting company is 'Reach the maximum number of people in the market', horizontal growth is the best course.

The 'flatter' the organisation, the more it remains outward-directed. By keeping things small, the company is more likely to ensure that the new consumer encountering the brand is treated in a personal and sensitive manner. Those already part of the following will be assured that their brand remains interesting and fresh.

Chapter 9

Competition: The New Ball Game

The arrival of concepting is beginning to radically change the nature of competition. The main thrust of the change is the elimination of traditional branch boundaries, with significant implications for companies taking traditional approaches, though concepting companies also have to adapt to the new environment they represent.

9.1 Classical marketing underestimates concepting

In the world of classical product development, when one company comes up with an innovation, it usually does not take long for the competition to study the new product and reproduce it. In most lines of business this is a matter of a few months – even less time is required if the initial innovations are cosmetic: anyone can copy a new custard or a peach-flavoured tea or turn out an 'environmentally friendly refill pack'. Such 'me-too' responses are not limited to physical products. For instance, a company's pricing (all too often down-pricing) or its distribution channels can also easily be copied.

To concepting companies, there is an advantage to the fact that their competition is often taking this unidimensional approach to marketing. Obsessed by product-oriented and market-segmentation thinking – 'the market for dry dog food', 'the liquid detergent segment', 'the market for men's underwear fashions' – they aim for market leadership. However, not everyone can be a market leader. The marketing solution has been to divide and redefine markets so that the company can claim leadership. In effect, a number one position is conveniently attained through market segmentation: a company thus can claim supremacy, for example, in liquid detergents for sensitive colour fabrics.

However, companies that enjoy seeing themselves as specialists in segment 'x', 'y' or 'z' are seriously blinkering themselves from what really matters: namely, the consumers. They abuse the notion of a 'market' by overstretching its definition to describe what are actually little more than accumulations of product categories. In their enthusiasm for segment statistics they lose sight of the consumer. They also tend to underestimate the competition of companies taking a different approach, and are blinded to the possibilities of imagining other markets – one for a brand, for example – beyond their tidy segmentations.

Apart from being initially underestimated by competitors, concept brands have the further advantage, as we have seen, of being very difficult to compete against using imitation. Initially, in particular, the visions are not always completely 'clear', so that the competition has a hard time trying to copy and incorporate into their market-segment thinking. Imagine trying to take on Ikea's concept, for example. In any case, as we have also seen, consumers do not tend to take too well to concept imitators.

The story of the Swatch concept brand is illustrative of the problems competitors face when trying to deal with concepting companies. The competition's initial response to the Swatch watch was not untypical: it simply did not take it seriously. Many in the technically oriented watch and jewelry establishment even scoffed at what they considered plastic play things, and accused its makers of mocking a serious trade. As it turned out, of course, the Swatch concept was a masterful move on the part of the Swiss watch industry, which was in disarray since it began losing ground to Japanese competition in the 1970s.

In fact, the first Swiss response to the foreign competition came in 1979, with the introduction of the *Delirium* model. This was the thinnest, most technically refined and simplest (in terms of number of components) watch in the world. It represented perhaps the last great cosmetic innovation rescue attempt. As such, it flopped: consumers stayed away in droves.

The industry found itself in a serious crisis and resolved to unite its forces in the SMH (Swiss Corporation for Microelectronics and Watch-making Industries). The association then decided to radically change the industry's approach: in effect, it turned to concepting. The result was the Swatch concept, the concept statement of which would, I believe, express the perspective of 'continuous innovation, provocation and fun'.

The Swatch watch was introduced in 1983. Made of plastic and available in an enormous variety of styles and colours, it was also equipped with a top-rate timepiece and was priced as a 'commodity'. Swatch was thus able to avoid 'competing' in the traditional watch market presented in the world of upscale, glossy magazines. Instead, Swatch presented itself as an accessible fashion brand, which constantly adjusted to the fast-paced, changing times. Swatch had created its own world – 'unglossy', young and whimsical.

The company has faithfully stuck to its concept, as can be verified by visiting its internet site at www.swatch.com. At first, the traditional watch industry did not take Swatch seriously. Some retailers even refused to add the 'plastic thing' to their selection. This did not bother Swatch in the least. It sought out non-traditional outlets – e.g. fashion, jewelry, stereo and computer equipment stores – and even opened its own stores. The company also started publishing annual catalogues, which were so well designed that they have – along with the watches – become collectors' items among the brand's following.

Swatch has become the most successful watch concept ever. It has sold more than 200 million watches, making SMH the world's largest watch producer. The Swiss have made an astonishing comeback. What is particularly remarkable about this story is that it involved having to make a huge mental shift from a traditional focus on technical competence to a concept focus, in which technical aspects are placed on a secondary plain. SMH's co-founder, Nicolas G. Hayek, still the company's CEO, demonstrated enormous capabilities in communicating the concept to the Swiss watch industry and was quick to exploit the concept's field with other products, like telephones and, lately, even the Smart car.

Hayek is not the only one who is laughing last and best: Virgin's Richard Branson, BSO's Eckard Wintzen and many others would be members of the proverbial chorus.

9.2 Branch incompatibility becomes concept compatibility

We have seen that the secret of concept brands is that they stand for something far beyond the actual product in the eyes of their following. Each brand has a unique vision and philosophy that is consistently conveyed in all its behaviour. The resulting autonomy of the brand with regard to products allows its logo or badge to be used on products that, from the perspective of traditional marketing, would be considered branch incompatible.

The logo, of course, is *the* symbol of the concept. In a flash, it conveys the brand's message to the consumer. Nike's swoosh, Swatch's Swiss flag, Virgin's artsy signature, all these examples immediately evoke a certain feeling. Not that any of these logos are particularly attractive or indeed original. In my view, more aesthetic ones can be found, while variations of the same themes certainly exist – bow-like logos, such as Nike's swoosh, are used by companies worldwide. The difference, of course, is that Nike's logo elicits the brand's concept, which has been built up in the public's mind over time – its vision of persistence, self-confidence, aspiration and performance. The cumulative effect of the brand's behaviour has created this association.

As the concept brand and its association with a particular meaning strengthens, the company can begin to add new products to its field. Nike began with training shoes, which were followed by athletic clothing, and then leisure (non-athletic) apparel. Soon, they will probably close their clothing line by adding jeans and underwear to their selection. Another real possibility is that Nike, on the basis of its contract arrangements with top athletes and teams, could enter the satellite television business, computer games and so on.

However, when it comes to these 'branch-incompatible' activities, perhaps no concepting company outdoes Virgin. Starting out in mail-order record sales, the Virgin brand field now includes musical production, record stores, studios, airlines, travel, interactive computer games, vodka, cola-drinks and much more. These Virgin companies have repeatedly won acclaim as the best and most customer-friendly organisations (maybe 'customer-active' would be more appropriate). Under the banner of the Virgin concept statement of rebelliousness, they are known for their drive and a hunger to take on new challenges. This naturally motivates the employees, who usually work in 'lean' organisations – a refreshing alternative to Virgin's competitors, so often smothered in bureaucracy. The consumer, in turn, enjoys the dynamic organisations and, incidentally, sees the results in better products and service (Virgin Airlines has won the Airline-of-the-Year Award three times running). However, most importantly, people identify with the concept; they like Virgin, and they are more than willing to let themselves be carried along with the flow of challenges that Richard Branson dares to tackle.

Caterpillar for its part is a good example of a brand from a traditional, technical sector that has been transformed into a concept brand, thereby creating a whole new concept field encompassing completely unrelated branches. The company's heavy excavation equipment and fork-lift trucks, with their distinctive yellow and black colour scheme, are well-known to everyone in the road-building and construction businesses. However, the Caterpillar brand made a quantum leap when, a few years ago, an entrepreneur bought the rights to use it for other kinds of products. What was purchased, in effect, was the right to turn it into a concept brand. Now there are Caterpillar shoes, leisure-wear, backpacks and so on. The concept is based on the original toughness and ruggedness associated with the traditional business – e.g. the products are made of heavy canvas. Caterpillar's core group were the young adults who felt they identified with the construction workers themselves. Soon, however, the following came to include other consumers, particularly adolescents. Indeed, the concept statement, which could be summed up as: 'honesty and straight-forwardness for men who literally move mountains', is appealing to a rapidly burgeoning following, including girls and women.

Cigarette brands, in response to advertising restrictions, have been forced to develop other product categories to carry their brand messages – either on their own or by selling the brand rights to others. For example, Pall Mall Clothing Company and Marlboro Classic are widely distributed in leisure-wear clothing stores; and Peter Stuyvesant has its own travel agency, which it uses to promote its 'world of Peter Stuyvesant' concept quite literally: the agency can get you to 'Stuyvesant' cosmopolitan spots all over the world.

Sanex is another example, though its field is a little narrower. Apart from a washing powder, Sanex is a deodorant, a skin cream and a soap. The concept stands for something like: 'naturalness, no-frills and no chemical additives when it comes to your skin care'. The Sanex success illustrates that concepting is also effective in the world of fast-moving consumer goods. All that is needed is good insight into people's needs.

These examples raise a question: How is Nielsen supposed to calculate the Sanex 'market-share', for example? I suppose the answer would be that Sanex cuts through all the traditional market segments and possesses only a few percentage points in each. As we have seen, this is of little consequence from a concepting perspective. The point is not to achieve impressive percentage numbers in each of these segments, but to attain the widest possible following for the concept – if they are spread out over many sectors, that is fine. Ultimately, what matters is that the company's performance is strong. In the process, the company's morale and culture are solid and healthy: instead of spending its communication resources on the tedious and inefficient battles with its larger competitors in every segment, it focuses on communicating the natural, pure concept contained in everything carrying its logo – sun-screen is probably next on the Sanex product list.

Dozens of other examples could be added to these examples of products in concept-brand fields: from Diesel and Boss perfumes to Harley Davidson furniture, not to speak of the huge field that is the Walt Disney brand, perhaps the world's largest concept brand. From a management perspective, what they all share is the challenge they present to the all-too-common recommendation consultants make to their struggling clients: 'Stick to your "core business"'. True, for companies that can still achieve distinctive value on the basis of genuine innovations this is sound advice, but the others I feel have to change their approach.

Another way of putting it is that these companies should make *concepting* their core skill and stick to *that*. The difference, of course, is that concepting-companies' core businesses are unrelated to products, being based on the communication.

9.3 Competition opens up to all

We have seen that there are a number of concept brands that are developing in today's market – a tendency, I believe, that will inevitably grow stronger in the years to come. The reason is simple: as the variety of goods and services successfully marketed under concept-brand fields grows, the nature of the business competition will change – traditional companies will probably have to take up concepting to compete and survive, while concepting companies themselves have to remain alert.

Nestlé's Nespresso brand offers a good example of the threat posed by concepting (in this case employed by a long-established multinational) to traditional market players. The Nespresso conveys the modest concept that we can spoil ourselves at home with fine coffee, just as well as we can with a glass of Armagnac or a good cigar. The coffee is packaged in little vacuum-packed cups, the colour of which indicates the blend. The coffee is sold exclusively to people who are Nespresso 'members', that is, who have ordered the special Nespresso espresso machine. The vacuum-packs – which by the way can be ordered by phone 24 hours a day – can only be used on Nespresso machines. In the Netherlands alone, 13,000 people purchased one of these machines for their homes in 1997. In effect, Nestlé had placed coffee machines under the brand's field, created a new following in the market, and as a result presented a serious and unexpected challenge to traditional coffee-machine producers like Philips, Krups, Braun and Illy.

Let us take a look at another example: blue jeans. Today, many of the brands in strong positions have their origins in traditional, product-oriented businesses – e.g. Levi's, Wrangler and Lee. However, recently these companies have had to deal with formidable concept-brand competitors, like Diesel, Pall Mall, Marlboro and others. Furthermore, there are very probably more on the way: nobody would be surprised if a jeans line were to be introduced by Virgin, Nike or even Ben & Jerry's. Any of these would have a good chance of creating a following among consumers.

From a traditional business perspective these cases reveal a scary reality: the competitive attack can come from *any* side. Often the only way out is to change – unable to beat the competition, Philips and Krups, or Levi's and Wrangler, might have to join them, by transforming themselves into concepting companies.

Concepting companies themselves, of course, have also to be constantly nimble and alert. When Boss makes the decision to add beautifully designed appointment books and fountain pens under its brand, it will threaten Filofax. However, the latter could, in turn, take its concept – 'helping to organise business and personal life as efficiently and as stylishly as possible' – into the leather goods market, by marketing briefcases, portfolios and other office accessories. Filofax's concept would fit in perfectly here.

Concepting, a product of our communication-oriented age, therefore introduces a new style of business competition. From one based on the qualitative performance of production and sales companies in predefined markets, competition will be based on *communicating concepts*. Concepts that radiate the most integrity and are communicated most authentically will be the most appealing and successful. They will be the victors in the battle for followings. Indeed, with concept statements in hand with openness, patience, creativity, nimbleness and consistency, many concepting companies are enjoying impressive growth.

9.4   Conditions for 'concepting' existing brands

Many of the concepting companies we have discussed did not actually start out as such. Nike and Benetton were originally developed from existing organisations, just as Virgin began as an ordinary mail-order company. Obviously, their example shows that this transformation is certainly possible; one need not start from scratch. However, they also reveal that a number of conditions are required for the transformation:

- If a brand is to be 'concepted', if you will, it needs to have a *reasonably neutral, untainted image*. This tends to be the case if it has not been communicated too much – for example, if it has not gone through the grind of innumerable positionings and repositionings. Paradoxically, this means that brands that were laggards in the marketing race have an advantage in a concepting context. Diesel, for example, before 1990 had hardly been advertised. On the other hand, brands that have already engaged in endless marketing battles have, in my view, little chance of succeeding: their image has already been tainted by confusion and weakness. Any attempt to transform such a typecast brand into a concept brand would very likely meet with consumer incredulity and ridicule.

- The brand leadership must have an *open-minded attitude* with regard to the outside world. It must also be able to take an unprejudiced view of the company's practices and market performance. It cannot consider any existing company traditions or structures, such as production plants and departments, as untouchable and sacrosanct. A management team of engineers, too enamoured of their R&D laboratory or production processes, is an unlikely candidate for the necessary mind-shift to concepting.

- Sufficient managers must *champion the concepting idea* and be willing to support it unequivocally. Indeed, these people will constitute the beginnings of a concepting team.

- The above individuals must have *unconventional attitudes and behaviour*. They should be up-to-date leaders who are good communicators, both with employees and the outside world.

- The entire organisation needs to *adjust to the new concept*. Leaders need to be acutely aware of the fact that this will probably be their toughest challenge ever and they will need to be persistent. They will start modestly, working with small core groups of consumers – their crucial, early brand ambassadors. They need not worry about existing customers: provided they are treated well, they will not just turn their backs on the company – they might even feel their trust in the brand has been confirmed if they see it taking positive steps.

Companies that meet these conditions will, in short, have a good chance of turning around. By making a fresh start on the basis of concepting, they will place themselves firmly in the communication-oriented age.

Chapter 10

A New Management Philosophy

The management practices and philosophy of a concepting company naturally differ from those of traditional models. The companies need different staff capabilities and the managerial skill to avoid certain dangers to which concept brands are particularly vulnerable.

10.1 From production, to sales, to marketing, to communications

A company's particular history, sector and the surrounding business culture are all determinants of the type of management it will have.[1] Take the example of Philips. After having invented the light-bulb in 1891, Gerard Philips went into business to produce and sell the new product. As an inventor and engineer, the main question in his mind was technical: How to develop the systems to produce as many light-bulbs as possible? Five years later, his 18-year-old brother, Anton, joined the company as head of sales. A much more extroverted man than his older brother and a skilled negotiator, he would ultimately become Philips' public 'face'. The family company soon evolved a dual-management system, under which the technical and sales capabilities were separated.

---

1. See Evolution of Entrepreneurship table on page 115.

Philips actually took this organisational step sooner than comparable companies at the time. Their management's reluctance was perhaps understandable: an engineer, for example, who comes up with an invention at the age of 30, and manages to expand his company rapidly under his leadership, is not, at the age of 40, going to be predisposed to create a sales directorship at his side. He is likely to be very proud of his technical accomplishments and believe that they are the key to his success. At first, in the beginning of the product cycle, this position is appropriate and tenable. However, once competitors start producing the same product, strong sales management is needed if long-term growth is to be ensured.

Companies that began exporting tended to realise sooner than others the need to give sales a more prominent position, since export success demanded that they find the best local sales staff. This was especially true after the Second World War, when production facilities were set up abroad, as exemplified in multinational companies like IBM, Heineken, Volkswagen and Unilever. Since they established operations in countries where they were usually one among few players, these sales-oriented organisations developed strong local positions. Sales staff abroad enjoyed much more power and freedom than their counterparts in the home countries, whose activities were under far tighter head-office control.

Thus multinationals tended to have management structures in which the sales perspective had as much representation as the production and technology perspective, even though the sales perspective was primarily a feature of foreign operations. By the mid-1950s, this convenient balance often degenerated into decision-making tugs-of-war between the central organisation and local subsidiaries. The struggle reflected the end of the halcyon days of booming growth: as long as sales figures abroad were terrific, no one in the home office was inclined to bother interfering with the sales departments. However, when figures worsened, internal battles raged, as the different departments blamed each other for the situation.

The struggle marked the beginning of more of a marketing orientation – Kotler introduced the term 'marketing' in 1956.

Naturally, for most companies it took many years before the idea took root. It began in the fast-moving consumer products and slowly spread to others. Indeed, Procter & Gamble was the first multinational company to make the discipline of marketing a fully fledged part of company strategy in each and every area where it had established a subsidiary. Other branches took a lot longer to catch on: e.g. business-to-business marketing and non-profit organisation marketing is relatively recent.

Even when marketing was introduced to companies, the transition from a basic sales orientation was not always clear-cut. In most corporations top management was in the hands of engineers in their 50s, and occasionally included younger people with sales experience acquired in foreign operations. In fact, in most companies marketing began as a modest staff function performed by a handful of people. Within the company they preached the four Ps and claimed to have a better overall perspective than the engineers or the sales directors, but they were not always persuasive.

Perhaps this arrogant attitude explains why the marketing men sometimes took so long to gain any appreciable access to management. Sales heads who had only just gained their places in the board rooms naturally regarded their area of expertise as all-important for continued growth, and kept the new 'theoreticians' at a distance. In fact, only after some serious internal battles did marketing gain a management standing comparable to sales – indeed, in some companies this battle has still to be won. In the case of Philips, it still seems to be raging, though the exclusive, family-based, technology-sales focus only recently made space for a market orientation. The Dutch aircraft manufacturer Fokker unfortunately never made the shift, and paid heavily for it with bankruptcy.

KLM is an example of a company that quickly adjusted its management structure and philosophy to changing market conditions. In the 1980s, Jan de Soet became the company's CEO. Chosen for his background as head of marketing and advertising, he fully recognised that service- and market orientation were the most important and distinctive factors for ensuring further corporate growth, just as important as the technology and skills required to keep planes in the air, to set up and run foreign sales operations – after all, the company's serious competitors performed equally well in these areas.

Some companies during the 1980s actually went so far as to completely subordinate sales to marketing. In my view, this is excessive since it often meant that marketing became too theory oriented and lost touch with market realities. Fortunately, the pendulum today seems to be swinging back and a better marketing–sales balance is more common. In fact, over the last few years, the most common approach has involved multi-disciplinary management teams. The particular focus of the corporation then becomes a function of the company's history and the strength of the different management-team members' personalities.

Over the last ten years, a new area of expertise – communications – has also begun to bid for management positions. Again, it will take time for top management to recognise the importance and relevance of the new orientation for their company. Curiously, it has frequently been those companies that trail the 'fast movers' in the area of marketing that have made the greatest strides in bringing in a communication perspective into top management – again, suggesting the advantage of not being 'encumbered' by previous success. Companies that fared relatively poorly in marketing moved fast: e.g. Canon, Rank Xerox and IBM. Service companies provide other good examples in this context. Having limited themselves to public relations, and practically ignored marketing, they actually fostered the communications capabilities useful in our post-marketing period. At a time when consumers are keener than ever about the mentality and behaviour of the corporation behind a brand, these corporations, whose names are their brand names, have a great opportunity to take advantage of this situation.

10.2 Concepting leaders

Just as concepting is increasingly becoming the only effective response to changes in many markets, so too is the communications function becoming indispensable in top corporate management. Indeed, I believe it is the most important new area of management, and I think most companies will realise this over the next few years. Communications managers will come to play a far greater, more balanced role along with other management-team members. Just how important this role becomes will depend on the line of business, what phase in its life cycle the company finds itself in, how visionary the owners are, and of course how pugnacious the communications managers are.

However, we have seen that companies with a long tradition have trouble developing concept brands – the 'world of Marlboro', for example, was a chance discovery; it was not planned, but was cleverly picked up on and developed as the brand's leading concept. We have also seen how Nike, Diesel and Benetton evolved very quickly into concept brands because their leaders were more than just the technically oriented founders of their companies. BSO and The Body Shop, on the other hand, were concept brands from the start, based on the visions of their founders.

These concepting leaders are more often than not great communicators. They have great vision, entrepreneurial spirit and sensitivity to what makes people 'tick'. That is why they seem able to see what others cannot. They start their businesses based on the belief that their concept stands a very good chance of appealing to large groups of people in the long term. They are frequently graduates of the school of hard knocks that are the large corporations. After failing to convince management of the value of their concepts and of communications they became disillusioned. Realising that their chances of convincing the technicians, salesmen, marketers and accountants are slim, they set off on their own.

Concepting leaders actually look different from traditional managers; they have a distinct style. In contrast to the engineer with his white smock and high forehead, the overly amiable and talkative salesman and the blue-suited marketing man, they remind one more of a pop artist, academic sociologist or left-leaning politician. Nothing is too off-beat for them, as evidenced by the three-day growths sported by Richard Branson, Eckart

Wintzen and Renzo Rosso. Take a look at the perpetually casual, jeans-clad Eckart Wintzen, and ask yourself whether any self-respecting computer-industry millionaire would have dared to walk around like that even ten years ago.

These individuals can be seen as archetypes of a new sort of leader who does not manage using organisational plans – whether drafted with the help of management consultants or not. Rather, he or she manages through intuition and communication. They think and feel organically, not systematically. Their vision is multi-dimensional, and they regard their organisational model more as a result than as a condition of success. They dare to quickly change course if necessary. Since they are concept oriented, their tendency is not to judge a department on the basis of its profit performance. They accept that each department is a part of the whole and that some things can turn out to be more expensive than originally hoped or expected. Such costs are seen as investments in long-term brand development.

Most of all though, they are great communicators. They walk around the company's facilities, talking and listening to people. They have the skill to convince others and to sweep them up in their visions. This quality is also helpful in external communications: they rarely need PR advisers. They are gifted with the ability to convey their vision to large groups of people, in a simple and straightforward way. They also have an uncanny knack of knowing exactly where they need to be and when: with their potential following or their media.

However, they do have a weakness, which they share with preceding generations of managers. It concerns a frequent inability to recognise that the brand development requires the presence of people with talents other than theirs.

10.3 The dangers of sectarianism and dependence

Concepting leaders are exposed to two particular dangers, both of which are related to their central role in their enterprises; and both of which can spell the end of their brand.

The first danger is that, flushed with their early success, concepting leaders believe they can go it alone. In doing so, they run the risk of turning themselves into sectarian-like leaders with all the stultifying effects one might expect. If a concept is the brain-child of a particular individual, who then goes on to become the brand's 'face', this can limit the company's prospects, particularly if the 'guru' cannot or will not share his or her role with others. Their realisation of their ability to draw large groups of people can go to their heads. Believing their own publicity, they feel invulnerable and become convinced that they alone can carry the concept. This can have a number of deleterious effects on the healthy expansion of the brand, as the leaders can become inward oriented, distant and deaf to criticism, thus posing obstacles to the development of new leaders and growth.

Benetton's case is interesting in my view because it is an example of a concepting leader who loses his bearings in this way and then manages to regain them at the urging of the public and management partners.

The Benetton family cherishes its privacy; which is not the case with Oliviero Toscani, their former campaign photographer. As a result, and because of his seminal role in the company's campaigns, I believe Toscani is, in effect, the leader of the Benetton concept, built on the foundations of the advanced, well-oiled, Italian ready-made clothing company. He had virtually free rein to develop his personal (visual) concept entirely on his own. At a certain point, however, Toscani started believing too much in his own image – he started becoming a little sectarian. He drifted away from the original concept and distanced himself from the brand's following. When his campaign turned more and more into an Aids campaign (however well intentioned) things started unravelling. Although the following believed in the brand's tradition of provocation, the excessive hammering at the Aids issue went too far: Toscani had overstretched the concept in my view. Although the consumer is certainly sensitive to Aids, he or she does not want to be confronted with it on a daily basis. It was too much, for instance, for the consumer who simply wanted to buy a new summer dress for her six-year-old daughter.

In the mid-1990s this led to damaging public controversy and to drop-outs amongst Benetton's following. Here and there, there were signs that sales were flagging and a number of franchisees – who depend on Benetton for the proper maintenance of the brand – rebelled and demanded changes. Things quietened down for a while and there were rumours that Benetton and Toscani would part ways. However, they eventually, and none too late, managed to come to terms and returned to the brand's original concept. In April 2000 the two finally parted ways; it will be interesting to see whether the company can keep the Benetton concept alive without its originator.

The second danger relates to the overdependence of a brand on the person of its leader. Even if he or she brings in complementary capabilities to run the organisation properly, by remaining the 'face' of the brand, the leader runs the risk of leaving it adrift if, for whatever reason, he or she departs. There is a difficult balance to strike in such instances, since the person of the leader is often a significant boost to the communication effort. This is the case, as we have seen, with Virgin's Richard Branson. Virgin *is* Richard Branson; and Richard Branson *is* Virgin. He regularly appears in the international media, whether piloting hot-air balloons or participating in ocean sailing races. What happens, however, if one of these days he is killed in an accident, or decides to retire to the Bahamas, and Virgin has to do without him? Although identification of a brand with its creator can be, at first, a good thing, after a while, once the company has taken off and established itself, it hangs like a sword over its destiny.

Phil Knight of Nike avoided this problem altogether by having star athletes embody the Nike concept. Most consumers probably do not even know who Phil Knight is, but everyone has heard of Michael Jordan and Ronaldo – the advantage of this approach of course is that it is easily refreshed: as the new stars appear they can easily be incorporated and the old ones dropped.

The solution of Diesel's Renzo Rosso, despite his activities in the worldwide lecture circuit, is to have his designers and other key employees step into the limelight as creators and active promoters of Diesel's colourful brand. Diesel would not be lost without him.

10.4   Hiring and nurturing concept carriers

We have seen that, as the brand following expands, the concepting company needs more people to convey and maintain the concept and its accompanying business culture. It is also necessary to have the right people in order to keep the streams flowing internally on the right course. For this reason, concepting companies, more than their traditional counterparts, need to pay particular attention to the character types of the new people they bring on-board, whatever their role and level in the organisation. Are they all – even administrative personnel – communication-oriented? Do they fit into the informal culture? Are they self-starters, initiative-takers who need few rules and direction from up above? Are they good generalists? Do they fit in well with the brand's mentality (which does not mean that they need to have exactly the same mentality)?

Naturally, the concepting company's leader realises that not everyone can or should be a sort of brand clone – that could certainly create a sectarian, if not fundamentalist, group. On the other hand, he or she is aware that there is a need for what might be termed 'concept carriers' in various positions at every level of the company's organisation. This is the case of every good concepting company I know of. The concept carriers' importance becomes obvious in the unfortunate event that a couple of them decide to leave: the motivation of those left behind can be seriously damaged. The trick is to select employees carefully and to motivate them in such a way that a number of them will naturally emerge as, in effect, informal 'mini-leaders'. Concept carriers are not generally available in the labour market, though people with the attributes to become carriers are. The concepting company needs to find and hire them, and then provide the right atmosphere for them to grow into their roles.

Of course, authoritarian managers do not provide the appropriate atmosphere for the development of concept carriers. Democratic leadership and flat business organisations are the necessary ingredients to this end. The company structure should evolve organically. If organisational charts with functional task assignments are necessary, the leadership should do what it can to make them as unobtrusive as possible. This it can do through good internal communications, by developing collective activities, by promoting inter-departmental co-operation and by rotating employees and jobs.

The objective of the company's leadership is to have its employees' energy focused on the essence of the company, namely the brand's concept, rather than on their own individual areas or departments. The more this happens, the more people will be able to manage themselves. They will draw in others to become carriers. The truth is, this is more important for a company's continuity in this communication-oriented age than buildings and customers.

10.5   From product managers, to brand managers, to concept managers

The growth of concepting raises the question as to whether there is still a place for a marketing manager and a product manager in this sort of corporation. The answer is: Yes, as long as they can adapt and become what I would call *concept managers*.

The product manager was appropriate when consultation with the factory and the packaging designer was necessary: the advertising agency was given a briefing on what the product had to offer. The initial 'P' in the marketing mix got all the attention. When added values came into their own, the figure of the brand manager emerged, particularly in the case of international brand-name producers whose ambition was to disseminate a single brand image worldwide. This manager was responsible for positioning the brand, and almost all his or her attention was directed at the fourth P in the mix: Promotion.

With the shift to a stronger communication orientation, different perspectives and skills are needed. Whether or not an individual can adapt to the 'softer' communications approach depends largely on his or her talents and background. To date, marketing people have tended to come from economics and other analytical educational backgrounds. The question is whether these qualities are appropriate in companies that are governed increasingly by intuition and emotion. Communications is more of a psychological or sociological field: a *people* field, if you will. This is going to be more and more the case in companies wanting to develop concept brands. Indeed, I believe that, ultimately, formal education and training will become less and less important, since our communication-oriented era relies more heavily on creativity, entrepreneurship and communication talent.

The future belongs to the concept managers and to communicators. I should add, however, that such terms are hardly ever used by the concepting companies mentioned in this book. The reason is these companies tend to work with concepting teams, containing a mix of entrepreneurial, creation, marketing, sales and communication talent. As concepters, team members jointly deliberate on how to launch a brand on the market and nurture its expansion. The good candidates for these (generalist) roles may have one or two of these talents, but no one person can have them all. Concepting is a team sport – preferably with small teams, as we have seen. With production and implementation elements of the marketing tasks (telemarketing, sales-force management, etc.) outsourced, small teams are feasible.

10.6   Merging concept brands is to suffocate them

Concept brands require autonomy and separate treatment if they are to prosper. They are fragile and need careful handling. They do not fare well when they are managed in a group with others or when under the power of people who are unfamiliar with their concepts and behaviour. These threats often come as a result of concepting companies being purchased by or merging with others. Indeed, more often than not, these mergers and acquisitions sound the death knell for the concept brand.

The initial threat, of course, is that the new management of the newly acquired concepting company might be tempted by the idea of imposing its culture and philosophy on the merged unit, as a whole. This could seriously damage its concept brands and weaken its concepting capability in general.

The more common threat relates to occasions in which management embarks on efficiency drives – a frequent occurrence in post-merger situations. The temptation is to pool activities and operations – e.g. logistics, administration and purchasing – of a number of brands as a cost-saving measure. The short-term effects of such moves are often positive, and are duly reflected in the company's results. The question is whether the cost of the damage that inevitably occurs to the carefully cultivated concept brands will, in the longer term, outstrip the short-term gains. Once the concept brand is eroded, it is very difficult to re-establish – the same applies to the communicative power, morale, drive and enthusiasm of the concepting team itself. Actually, if a few of the veteran concepters decide to leave as a result of a merger, the alarm bells should start ringing in the new parent company's headquarters. We have seen that if key people leave, the concepting team's motivation is vulnerable; this is all the more so when those who stay have to adjust to the guidelines of a new culture.

Even if nobody leaves and the new owners are enthusiastic about the concept brands they have acquired, it is always doubtful whether they will have what it takes to manage them well. However well-intentioned they are, they will face the huge challenge of understanding and 'feeling' the brand alongside those who not only conceived it, but also accompanied it throughout its life.

Consider the hypothetical, though not unlikely, situation in which the concept brand Corona is bought by brewing-giant Heineken. Let us assume that, in the interest of economy, sales responsibility for Corona is given to the manager who is also responsible for Heineken's other brands. The sales-person would thus have the new brand added to a number of other brands in his or her portfolio. Corona would be bundled in with the others and not have its own, dedicated representative (ambassador) to convey the Corona concept in the market. This would seriously threaten Corona. The skills required to create a concept-brand following are very different from those needed simply to sell a product. It requires strong motivation, understanding and identification with the brand; no one representative could direct these capabilities into more than one brand effectively.

In general, the odds are good that the staff of the company doing the taking-over will not have the characteristics required to ensure the integrity and continuity of the acquired concept brands. Their company is likely to be a market leader, which, together with the fact that *they* are doing the taking-over, might make them a little too self-assured or even arrogant. The newcomers are often treated with a certain condescension and perceived as a group of 'amateur bunglers' (though an objective observer would have trouble deciding who has more to teach whom in such cases). Heineken offers an example of this: after the company took over Amstel many years ago, the new brand suffered 'second brand' status, being treated as a sort of step-child for years.

In another example, the implications for the BSO (now Origin) concept of Philips' takeover of the company were very uncertain for a long time. After the concepting leader, Eckart Wintzen, left, the two CEOs who followed him failed to continue his visionary leadership and Philips sold the company off.

However, final judgement in such cases must for the time being remain open, although, as a general proposition, it is worth remembering that mergers, unless very carefully managed, present a significant threat to concept brands. The new management should not be misled when they realise that the strength of these brands is founded 'only' in communications and their behaviour codes. The tendency among those not familiar with such brands is to underestimate the importance of these 'soft' elements. Moreover, with regard to the concepters themselves, the new management should not operate under the illusion that 'nobody is irreplaceable' – the better adage would be: 'Never change a winning team'.

In conclusion, my feeling is that if executives were clearly informed of the cost – in pounds and pence – of the talent drain, delays and deflated morale that often accompany mergers and acquisitions, they would engage in a lot fewer of them.

10.7 From multinational to 'multi-conceptual'

If a large multinational company happens to have a number of concept brands in its portfolio, and wants to ensure their health, it has to establish an organisational framework in which the brands can profit from being part of the whole while maintaining their own character.

Among other things, this means abandoning the notion that as many of its employees as possible need to be located in the same place, grouped, across brands, into specific departments: i.e. all the marketing people in one place, all the administrative people in another, and a separate spot for sales. Such a policy renders brands anonymous amidst the brand clutter: they take second place to corporate structure and process. However good the intention, this clustering is not a good idea. People engaged in concepting work better and more creatively when they are in close contact with individuals with other tasks and talents who are working on the same brand.

The exception to this, of course, relates to 'practical' tasks, such as production (if it is in-house) or administration, for which the case in favour of such departmental clustering is obvious. The goal of these activities is to deliver the highest-quality services – e.g. data processing, reports – at the lowest possible price, to the various (concepting) centres in the company. However, with regard to the concepting and entrepreneurial aspects of managing a brand – predominantly matters of communication – the tasks should be located in the separate concepting centres.

This means, for example, that if Heineken were to acquire smaller, international beer brands such as the Singaporean brand Tiger, then those in charge of their marketing and communication should be able to continue to enjoy the freedom to do their work independently from colleagues who are responsible for the Heineken brand. They should also be allowed to pursue their work in a location that is appropriate to their brands, as recommended earlier.

When the concepting centres are given their own 'space', an idealistic (not unrealistic), networking, flat 'non-organisation' should arise. The centres are, naturally, connected through an extensive, super-fast, digital network with the production, logistical and financial centres. Together they form a whole. Above ground, these connections are not obvious: each concepting centre has its own visible identity, carefully selected in line with the brand. Chosen by the concepters themselves, it is the ideal workplace and a 'communicative' reception space for consumers, buyers, suppliers, journalists and other groups.

The consumer's perception of the brand's 'home' is of primary importance. This is not the place where the traditional central role of the holding company is carried out; where the performance of the different business units, factories, subsidiaries and (eventually) concept centres are gathered, added up and analysed. In fact, the place where these tasks are performed takes on a lower profile under concepting. The drive to exhibit corporate power and importance through imposing architectural structures is diminished. This is not important. The only thing that shareholders are really interested in is performance. Under concepting, an unwieldy head office that has become notorious for its all-too-frequent reorganisations is a far less attractive proposition than the responsive, people-oriented structures of a concepting centre.

Which of these is the most realistic business scenario for 2010?

This one?

Euroworlds, a multinational, operates in 12 European countries and has three concept brands: Swatch, Davidoff and Virgin. In one of the countries, Euroworlds has its large, impressive head office, which houses its central services, such as control, (Euro)marketing, (Euro)sales, (Euro)communications and production. The name 'Euroworlds' is displayed proudly in huge neon letters on the building's roof.

The subsidiaries in each of the 12 countries have their own headquarters, which are small versions of the central office: their departments mirror those of the centre, while their buildings are crowned by the same 'Euroworlds' neon sign. The Swatch, Davidoff and Virgin brands are managed behind the scenes in these offices. All are handled according to the same corporate procedures, and all three brand operations produce the same standard daily, weekly or monthly reports for the head office. Euroworlds' people

Contd

are big travellers: tallying up hundreds of thousands of
kilometers annually, as they attend co-ordination meetings
throughout Europe. Meetings are important, as are procedures. Budgets are only drawn up after seemingly endless
tugs-of-war between the holding company and its subsidiaries
– often with the help of some very creative, collective
accounting. In this scenario, in short, all busy themselves
nicely, following procedures and fighting for turf.

Or this one?
Euroworlds is still the holding company. Swatch has a
concepting centre in Geneva, Virgin's floats on the Thames
in London and Davidoff's is located in Copenhagen. Each
displays its own brand on its roof. The centres have been
designed and decorated to receive the media and the
public. Communication with the brands' following –
through the internet, (house) European magazines, MTV,
CNN and whatever else fits the concept – takes place from
these centres. In the other countries there are smaller,
brand-based local satellites which have been established to
handle distribution, sales, customer service, etc. They also
take care of some local PR and communications. This
would entail, say, three small premises in a given country,
though such a presence would not necessarily have to be
built in every country. For instance, the Davidoff satellite
for the Netherlands, Belgium and Germany might be
situated, close to all three, in the Dutch town of Venlo. The
name 'Euroworlds' would not even appear in the
telephone directories of the 12 countries. Maybe the
holding company itself would be located, unobtrusively,
on the eighth floor of a faceless office building in Antwerp.
The outside world would not necessarily be aware of the
location of the production facilities themselves – in any
case, most production would be done by third parties and
delivered directly to their retailers.

Evolution of Entrepreneurship

Company type (Phase)	Focus within marketing mix	Company leadership	Ingredients for enterprise	Product development initiators	Communication concept	Consumer needs	Communication agency
Product-oriented (From ancient times)	Product	Engineer Craftsman	Raw materials Factory *Tangible*	Inventor • Genuine product development	Announcement • Explanation	Functional *Physical*	Ad space brokers • Placements in publications
Sales-oriented (From 1920s)	Price	Engineer + Sales director	Factory Storehouse Sales organisation	R&D force Salesmen • Genuine product innovation	Sales arguments: features, innovations and comfort • Comparison	Functional and convenience	Advertising studio • Development of advertising tools and sales support material
Marketing-oriented (From 1956: Kotler)	Distribution	Engineer + Business manager + Marketing director	Factory Storehouse Headquarters: marketing staff, sales department	Marketing Competition • Cosmetic innovation	Added value: cosmetic innovations and lifestyles • Association	Material: status, recognition	Marketing communication agency • Translation of messages into mass media Agency specialisation (PR, DM, SP, Design, etc.)
Communication-oriented (Starting ca 2000)	Communication	Communicator	Concept Communication Creativity Others outsourced *Intangible*	Concepters Visionaries Concepting agencies • Concepts	Concepts: visions, philosophies, mentalities • Behaviour	Non-material: philosophical/ idealism, experiences, self-realisation *Mental*	Concepting agency Concept development Co-entrepreneurship

Index